A GRAND
DINNER PARTY

Pauline Greenidge

A GRAND DINNER PARTY

Setting the Table for Employee Engagement Through Mergers and Acquisitions

A Grand Dinner Party
Setting the Table for Employee Engagement
Through Mergers and Acquisitions

www.paulinegreenidge.com

ISBN: 978-1537131047

Design and Layout by New Dimension Design

Copy Editing by Taija Morgan

Illustrations by George Sellas

Printed in USA

For Enid and Aldine

Table of Contents

PREFACE

Mergers and acquisitions are complicated business transactions that are occurring more frequently in today's business world. These types of business events are disruptive and impact employee productivity. Many books and articles have been written on the process of mergers and acquisitions. However, only a few of these specifically articulate the employee experience during these events. Even fewer describe what an actual merger or acquisition is like for employees and the steps an executive or business owner can take to manage and engage them through all of the phases of a merger or acquisition.

In 2009, I was privileged to be a part of the human resources team focused on managing employees through crucial integration stages that enabled the merger between Suncor and Petro Canada, two Canadian oil and gas giants. The merger of these two organizations resulted in an employee base of approximately 13,000 and was, at that time, the largest energy merger in Canadian history. As an HR professional, I learned a great deal about how incredibly difficult and complex it can be to manage employees through such a large business transaction. As an employee, for the first 18 months of the merger it was mentally, emotionally, and physically taxing. But that hard work was not without a positive outcome! My experience in that merger provided me with key insight into what is missing during mergers and acquisitions. That insight is that there is a need to have a thoughtful and deliberate plan to engage employees during mergers or acquisitions so effective business transformation can take place.

This book was written for business owners, executive teams,

and HR professionals who are in the planning stages of a merger or acquisition and want to realize and position the long-term value of an effective business transformation. The end goal of a merger or acquisition is to increase profitability, market share, opportunities, and growth—in essence, to transform. As an executive or business owner, you know how to make a deal, you might even know how you want to integrate your newly acquired assets and people, but have you planned for the transformation you seek? Planning ahead to properly engage your employees so they can help the organization achieve the desired transformation is the missing link in creating a successful merger or acquisition outcome. To transform an organization, executives and business owners need to have a clear vision, a solid business strategy, clearly defined values, and ways to measure results. Employees also need to understand and align with the vision strategy and values.

Within these pages, I describe practical actions executives and business owners can take to manage and engage employees through all the merger or acquisition phases. What makes this book different from others is that it highlights the two distinct requirements that are necessary to ensure a successful long-term merger or acquisition outcome:

1. The creation of a *Transformation Plan* that is deliberately designed early in the merger and acquisition process which gets employees focused and engaged quickly.

2. The engagement of a *Transformation Specialist* to develop a Transformation Plan that is customized for the organization as it progresses through the phases of a merger or acquisition.

Why are these two requirements so important? Why should a business owner or leader even care? It's important because a high percentage of these transactions fail. There has been much research done on the success—and mostly failure—of merger and acquisition transactions: *"Most research indicates that M&A activity has an overall success rate of about 50%—basically a coin toss"* (Sher, R., 2012). The consequences of creating a successful merger or acquisition are significant. The deal can enable or destroy the value of the newly created organization. Whatever the reasons for your organization deciding to merge or acquire are—to increase market share, revenue growth, economies of scale, or straight-up survival—it's imperative to recognize the knowledge, skills, and talents of the employees involved and have a plan to engage those employees to ensure the value of your investment is realized.

Throughout the book, I share highlights of my personal experience along with insights and advice about the importance of planning for employee engagement early in the merger and acquisition process. I frame this advice by using simple, yet powerful analogies. These analogies are based on the idea of throwing an elaborate dinner party. I use the idea of a dinner party because it highlights two key concepts I want executives and business owners to employ: *a mindset of invitation* and the *thoughtful planning* such an event requires. The title of this book, *A Grand Dinner Party*, reflects a better way, based on my experience, to purposely invite employees to engage and celebrate their role in the critical three phases of a merger—the Transaction (pre-deal), Pre-Transformation (integration), and most importantly, Transformation (post-deal). To complement my insights and advice, I have conducted a number of interviews with individuals from CEO-level to employee-level who have led or experienced a merger or acquisition. Their views are shared throughout the book.

The first two chapters, *What's Your Dinner Party Theme?* and *Who's Coming for Dinner?* speak to some of what employees will experience during the Transaction phase, or the time leading up to a merger or acquisition and after the initial announcement. These chapters detail some of the thoughtful preparation and planning required of executives and business owners immediately after a merger or acquisition takes place. *Welcome Your Guests* and *Setting the Table* are chapters that outline what can be done to help "on-board" employees and prepare them for the challenges of the pre-transformation process. The *What's on the Menu?* chapter describes the hard work required to make the transaction come to life and how to manage employees through it. Finally, *Dessert – Planning for Your New Culture* summarizes key points and concepts on how to best create the foundation of a strong and sustainable culture post-merger. Key ingredients in building that new and vibrant culture include values, community, a sense of belonging, opportunity, and growth.

I trust *A Grand Dinner Party* will provide you with straightforward and meaningful guidance as you embark on your merger or acquisition journey. I share my experience and observations in a simple way to help you achieve the merger success your business aspires to. Simplicity often creates profound results. John Maeda writes: *"Simplicity is about subtracting the obvious and adding the meaningful."* My sincerest wish is that *A Grand Dinner Party* does just that.

– *Pauline Greenidge*

TRANSACTION

CHAPTER 1

Mergers and Acquisitions Are Like a Grand Dinner Party

"Simplicity is the ultimate sophistication."
– Leonardo Da Vinci

Like Da Vinci, I am a believer that clarity is best achieved through keeping things simple. If you are an executive or business owner contemplating a merger, acquisition, or growth strategy, the metaphor of a grand dinner party is my way of simplifying the important steps required in managing and guiding employees through mergers and acquisitions more effectively. A grand dinner party is a structured and special event that typically has some importance and, most importantly, is *planned* for.

Most of us have fond memories of creating or enjoying a delicious meal with family and friends. When I bring people together for a meal, I usually have a reason or theme in mind when starting to plan an enjoyable dinner. Sometimes I plan my dinner party based on a specific dish I would like to make, or sometimes there's a theme I would like to create the meal around. Other times, it's about whom I would like to bring together to enjoy a well-thought-out meal. I give particular thought to the menu I would like to prepare that would complement the guests I plan to invite. The right mix of people with the right menu can create a delightful and memorable evening that friends, family, or special guests will remember for years to come. It doesn't matter if it is a formal dinner, a barbeque, or a potluck with the neighbours, there is something very special about sharing a meal with others that inevitably creates a sense of belonging and a connection. Even a regular middle-of-the-week meal with family sets the groundwork that allows us to share information and exchange ideas that build and strengthen relationships. Over time, that groundwork can become the foundation of a strong family unit, group of friends, or even business partnership.

So just how is a merger like a grand dinner party? During the planning stages of a dinner party, typically you:

- Establish the theme or reason for your party.

- Create the invitations to determine who is coming for dinner.

- Set the table.

- Welcome your guests.

- Serve them a great meal, including a delicious dessert.

All of these steps are taken to set the stage for dialogue, camaraderie, and a common celebration. What if we approached mergers or acquisitions with the same intent of inviting our employees to an occasion where they are considered important guests, where there is dialogue, camaraderie, and a reason to come together? To engage your employees during a merger, parallel the planning required for a dinner party in the following ways:

- **Create the Vision** – what's the theme or reason for the merger or acquisition gathering?

- **Create the Invitation** – what corporate values of the new company will attract and retain your new and existing employees?

- **Create the Welcome** – create an on-boarding plan to the new company for your new and existing employees.

- **Set the Table** – have a pre-transformation plan for managing the integration process.

- **Work Together** – decide what's on the menu for the new organization and how you will serve it; determining what processes, tools, and systems will be used in the new company.

- **Dessert** – create an inviting and sustainable foundation for your new culture.

The grand dinner party analogy has been specifically designed to highlight the steps that an executive or business owner can take to navigate their employees through the three phases of a merger or acquisition. These phases are the Transaction (pre-deal), Pre-Transformation (integration), and Transformation (post-deal). Transformation is the desired outcome, but long-term, dedicated attention is not typically paid to how transformation can actually be achieved. Planning for transformation seems like it would be a very important step executives and business owners should take, yet mergers fail more often than not due to the lack of a dedicated plan to navigate employees through the transaction, pre-transformation, and transformation phases of a merger or acquisition. If a merger or acquisition is on your company's horizon, a dedicated plan that is well thought-out and well lead is imperative: "[…] *firms that have a systematic approach to deal-making are more likely to be successful. Underlying this successful approach is the recognition of attention to many people-issues (a.k.a., human capital) that exist throughout the stages of mergers and acquisitions*" (Schuler, R. & Jackson, S., 2001).

My experience as an employee in one of Canada's largest energy mergers in corporate history has helped me formulate a simple but new idea for how to make the corporate merger or acquisition experience better. Mergers, acquisitions, and takeovers, are *not* going away. They will remain a key strategic lever that organizations will pull to achieve better business outcomes quickly. Why don't we start to consider mergers or acquisitions as an opportunity for celebration for employees and executives alike? We should challenge the norm and create a new way of approaching employee engagement in mergers or acquisitions.

A grand dinner party is a structured and special event that often has great importance. The invitations, guests, place setting, and seating are all there to set the stage for dialogue, good food, and a common celebration. What if we approached mergers or acquisitions with the intent of inviting our employees to a grand occasion where they are important guests? Simple idea, but imagine what it would be like if employees felt like they were welcomed into a grand occasion with all the pomp and circumstance that goes along with it? This isn't about being soft and squishy for no reason. *A Grand Dinner Party* is a metaphor for the steps to create the employee engagement that underpins and drives corporate alignment and sustainable business results.

One of the main reasons mergers or acquisitions fail is because executives and business owners don't invest enough time developing and executing a transformation plan for employees. Mergers or acquisitions and the path to transformation require a long and carefully thought-out journey. It's a worthwhile journey if you are prepared to follow some simple steps outlined in this book. The three merger or acquisition phases outlined below are designed to help guide executives and business owners in managing the employee experience.

Three Phases of a Merger or Acquisition

Transaction

The transaction phase occurs when an organization is actively creating the deal and doing the necessary homework to finalize it. This is when a company starts looking at the financials, assets, supply chain, and regulatory or legal issues pertaining to buying another company they wish to acquire to determine if a successful deal can be made. During this time, executives or business owners may engage only a few employees in key positions within legal, finance, and human resources to determine the viability of the deal and then take actions to make it come to life. In dinner party terms, this is where you decide the theme of your party and create an enticing invitation for the guests you plan to invite.

Pre-Transformation

The pre-transformation phase is the period of time directly following the transaction phase where the deal has been struck and it has been communicated internally and externally to all stakeholders. This is an extremely critical time in a company's merger or acquisition journey as it determines who will run the newly created organization. People, processes, and technology are the most significant areas that an executive or business owner needs to focus on during the integration. How each of these areas is impacted depends largely on whether one company is being taken over by another or if two organizations mutually decide to merge together and maintain elements of both companies. In reality, most mergers are takeovers where one company's way of doing business dominates and the other is absorbed over time. Once your invitation is sent, this is the part of your party where you welcome the guests to your home. It's important in this phase to ensure you have invited the right guests, set the right place settings, and that your guests know what's on the menu so they are prepared and can take part in the menu you are serving.

Transformation

Transformation is the achievement of the intended outcome of the transaction. If done properly, it can enable growth and opportunities for the new company and its employees. This is the phase of a merger or acquisition that is rarely given a continued, dedicated focus by executives or business owners. That is because true transformation takes time. The development of the new company's culture, values, and ways of getting the work done require deliberate and consistent attention over a span of many years to achieve. Transformation is the delicious dessert at the end of a fabulous meal. Like a vibrant, healthy culture, your guests will talk about it and want to enjoy it over and over again.

Mergers, acquisitions, and takeovers are reported in the media with increasing frequency. It is an important strategy that companies use to ensure their survival and future growth. In fact, many employees have experienced or will experience a merger or acquisition in their career, or some sort of corporate consolidation. What we rarely hear about is the impact that mergers and takeovers have on the employees who are involved. We hear about job cuts or massive layoffs, but that's usually the end of the story. What happens on the inside and its effects on employees is rarely revealed.

Initially, my reason for writing this book was to help reconcile my own feelings about the merger I experienced and to share that story with others so that they could see the experience for what it truly is: an opportunity. I believe that these significant and often disruptive corporate events present unique opportunities for individuals to grow personally and professionally. I want to inspire executives and business owners to consciously think about and participate in mergers or acquisitions in a better way.

While they likely consider the impact of these transactions on their employees, the focus of executives and business owners is to secure a successful business deal. What will make a more successful transaction is when an executive or business owner can make the deal *and* have a plan in place to manage the impact on their employees. Having a plan to manage the impact should also be a focus. The result is that executives and business owners will find their employees contributing and engaging more to achieve a successful merger or acquisition outcome. With a shift in perspective, executives and business owners can still make a merger or acquisition deal *and* maintain engaged employees to achieve the business results they desire.

The intent of *A Grand Dinner Party* is aspirational, and highlights ways executives and business owners can achieve a more successful merger or acquisition outcome by planning for it in a clear and purposeful way.

Simply put, if you don't plan for the transformation you wish for, the merger or acquisition will fail. To paraphrase from *Alice's Adventures in Wonderland, "If you don't know where you are going, any road will take you there"* (Carroll, L., 1865). To that end, I believe there should be a fresh mindset for employee engagement in mergers or acquisitions. That mindset is one of inviting employees to help transform their company and workplaces into something better.

"Be transparent about why you are doing the M&A. You don't want to lose your key people. Find a quick win to demonstrate the value of the deal and show you are moving forward. Measure your success and know your KPIs."

– Donna Garbutt, CEO, Maxxam Analytics

Key Insights

Mindset of Invitation

- Executives and business owners need to demonstrate a mindset of invitation by inviting employees to help transform their company and achieve intended business results.

An Employee-Engagement Plan is Critical

- It is critical for executives and business owners to have a plan to engage their employees through the various phases of a merger or acquisition. That plan has to be developed at the *very beginning* of any merger or acquisition being contemplated.

CHAPTER 2

What's Your Dinner Party Theme?

Suncor, Petro-Canada Announce Merger...

"*Appealing to Canadian nationalism, Suncor Energy Inc. and Petro-Canada said Monday that a proposed merger between the two oil players would create the country's largest energy company and provide the oil patch with protection against potential foreign buyouts.*"

– CBC News, March 23, 2009

Declare Your Vision

When orchestrating a large-scale change in your business, such as a merger or acquisition, the corporate vision of the new company needs to be declared immediately for three reasons:

1. Employees need to know why the merger or acquisition is happening and how it supports the vision.

2. Determining the vision identifies who should be invited to the dinner party.

3. Communicating how the merger or acquisition will unfold establishes clarity and transparency about what the merger or acquisition is trying to achieve.

If you are having a Mexican fiesta party, you don't want your preferred guests coming dressed for a black tie affair! Sounds simplistic, but in the merger or acquisition space, it can mean the difference between having a great vision with the wrong teams—employees and leaders without the right skills or abilities trying to execute on a strategy—or worse, having the wrong vision and strategy, and frustrating talented employees and stakeholders who are not engaged or able to carry out the strategy. When employees understand the reason behind the transaction, they can begin to engage in the transformation. It will help employees decide if they want to or can be a part of your dinner party going forward.

Declaring your dinner party theme or corporate vision early will help employees make key decisions for their future, help them determine the contribution they want to make to the newly created company, and, most importantly, help them decide whether or not their values align with the vision.

Ego Balanced with Pragmatism

"An architect imagines what if. A builder figures out how to. Great structures only emerge when the two work well together in pursuit of a shared vision."

– Simon Sinek

Executives and business owners need to exercise caution as they unveil their vision. The importance of a clear and concise vision is crucial, especially after the announcement of a merger or acquisition. It is one of the first ways leadership tells the employees what they need to be committed to. No one cares when a great vision is unveiled if it is impossible to achieve. Creating a vision and understanding how to implement that vision are not always complementary skills.

Vision is an organization's first attempt at expressing the type of culture they want to instill. As Thomas Edison tells us, *"Vision without execution is hallucination."* Highly skilled executive teams possess the rare ability to see that which is readily observable today, and balance it with the perception of what may happen in the marketplace in the future to use it to its advantage. Simply stated, great leadership acts as an organization's weigh scale, ensuring equilibrium between today's activities and tomorrow's opportunities. When creating a corporate vision, the up and down motion of balancing what is happening today with what is to be achieved tomorrow can be very challenging.

Mergers, acquisitions, and takeovers are becoming an increasingly common strategy to make a corporate growth vision come to life. The promise of reduced costs, more efficiency, increased cash flow, better asset mix, and raised shareholder value can be quite seductive as the company moves its fulcrum on the corporate weigh scale to maintain balance and enable growth and profitability. All too often, the pursuit of an acquisition or merger sounds like a great idea that offers many *possibilities* to an organization, but the *probability* of those possibilities actually becoming a successful venture is unlikely. In the 2001 McKinsey article, *Why Mergers Fail*, Bekier, Bogardus, and Oldham postulate that: *"Success is determined above all by the ability to protect revenue and to generate growth just after a merger. Those acquirers that get the balance wrong—plunging headlong into cost savings—may soon see their peers outstrip them in growth."*

And therein lies the challenge of successful execution of a merger or acquisition. The newly created corporate entity is likely larger and definitely more complex. Management of the joint assets and people require significant and careful review, care, and attention to maximize benefits. Establishing a new vision that inspires, honours employee contributions, and is motivating is not an easy task. The theme of your grand dinner party and the sequence of the events that follow should be clear to your guests. I can say with hand on heart that as an employee I could not have articulated the newly merged company's vision authentically because I was mentally stretched at the time with urgent tasks at hand that involved a lot of hard work. Corporate vision is a living thing. It should never be stagnant and must reflect the corporate values, the corporate mandate, and inspire and guide employees to feel proud of that vision.

When the Suncor/Petro-Canada merger was announced on March 23, 2009, the president and CEO of Suncor said, *"I don't know if it is a marriage made in heaven. But it is a match made in Canada"* (CBC News, Mar 23 2009). In retrospect, his statement was an honest and accurate perception of what was about to happen to the balance of Suncor's weigh scale. One of the most interesting things about combining two companies together—and why so many fail—is that no one *truly* knows what the balance will look like going forward.

You can plan, prepare, and create a clear path of what it *should* look like, but in the end, it is still an unknown. Like an on-line dating couple who get married, they take the plunge and are hoping to reap the benefits of mutual compatibility (merging), shared assets, and the promise of regular intervals of contentment (profits). Suncor and Petro-Canada had been dating for a long time and they almost wed previously in 1999, so when they finally created the "match made in Canada" it was the culmination of many years of courtship.

Ego balanced with pragmatism is the idea that executives and business owners must invest equal time on crafting the vision *and* planning for its execution in order to realize any real long-term benefits and maintain employee engagement. In order to craft your vision, you need to be clear as to whether or not you want to merge with, acquire, or take over another asset. This informs your strategy and the types of guests you will want and need to invite to your dinner party.

Mergers and Acquisitions

The use of the word *merger* is a business term that allows an organization to position themselves for one of two events: a takeover, or a plan of arrangement. Throughout this book, you will hear me refer to the joining of Petro-Canada and Suncor as a merger. Tory's LLP provided legal counsel to Petro-Canada in 2009, and in the document *Key Legal Considerations for Mergers & Acquisitions in Canada*, they describe those events as either:

1. Takeover bids.
2. Plans of arrangement.

A takeover bid is:

- *An offer to acquire shares of target directly from shareholders.*
- *Where some form of second-stage transaction will be required to obtain 100% of shares.*

A plan of arrangement is described as:

- *Single-step negotiated with the target and undertaken in accordance with the statutory requirements of the target corporation's governing statute.*
- *Where shareholder approval is required—threshold is typically*

2/3 of the votes cast at the special meeting.

- *Also requires court approval—determination of procedural and substantive fairness.*

- *Offers the most flexibility for tax planning and dealing with various classes of securities.*

The difference between a merger or an acquisition in practical terms: *"In a merger, two companies come together to create a new entity. In an acquisition, one company buys another one and manages it consistent with the acquirer's needs"* (Schuler, R. & Jackson, S., 2001). If your merger or acquisition is to ensure your company's survival, the speed and approach required to manage employee engagement will be quite different than if you are looking to make an acquisition for growth.

In my research, I found a multitude of articles, white papers, and books that detail the success factors for mergers or acquisitions. There are even more articles that describe the reasons why these ventures fail. In many of these writings, the reasons for merger failure are described as either the inability to remain nimble due to increased size, or a lack of cultural integration, or people issues. For example, in the Daimler-Chrysler merger that took place in the late 1990s, issues around cultural differences and the employees' understanding of the vision of the new company were not addressed properly.

"Take, for example, the union of Daimler [...] and Chrysler. That 1998 merger of equals created the giant German-American carmaker DaimlerChrysler. Just two years later, Jürgen Schrempp, by now in sole command, having seen off Robert Eaton, the former head of Chrysler, claimed that the term 'merger of equals' had been used only for 'psychological reasons,' thereby effectively acknowledging that equality was just a word used to sell the deal to Chrysler folk. It was a Daimler takeover. The marriage struggled on until May 2007,

when a divorce was announced" (Brew, A., 2014).

This merger ultimately failed because there was not a clear vision of the new company, and employees were not told in authentic terms what the value of the transaction was going to be or how they could contribute. There were two different cultures, located on two different continents, and their product offerings were quite different. Merging companies is an intricate, multi-faceted process laden with many pitfalls and opportunities for success. When employees are uncertain about the direction their company is taking, loss of productivity and rumours about what is happening will result. If these rumours or rumblings are not managed properly, they can cause confusion and misinformation at a time when an organization can least afford it.

Rumblings

Before an executive or business owner makes a decision to merge or acquire, there are many steps that need to be considered. These steps, when taken, are a reaction to what's happening in the business or marketplace at the time, and influence the direction and creation of a company's strategy. Decreases in share price as well as layoffs and work stoppages are typical reasons why a company will need to rethink or change its strategy. I refer to these reasons as Rumblings.

From my experience, this is typically how employees experience these changes in their company. Rumblings are business indicators or activities that lead an organization to change course and are often the precursor to a merger or acquisition. Rumblings are quiet, low vibrations that, when you hear them, you know something is there, but they are in the distance or not entirely discernable. Rumblings provide us with clues about what's ahead.

Whether the rumblings are under the hood of your car or in your organization, as an executive or business owner you need to be aware of your how your employees are experiencing them and create a strategy to manage them. They will occur whether you are working in a public or a private company. Your employees will experience these rumblings as changes in economics, layoffs, rumours, work slow-downs, and the frequent presence of the executive leadership or Board Members/Investors. As you read through each of the rumblings described, consider how these might be taking place in your own organization and what can be done to mitigate them with your employee base.

Regardless of the direction in which you want to take your company, you will be heavily engaged in the planning of these events. While you are doing so, many of the activities will not be visible to your employees and they may perceive the lack of corporate transparency as leadership deception. This deception is not intentional and is often unavoidable.

Leadership Deception – What Executives Can't Share

Leadership deception in this context is referring specifically to those things that executives or business owners won't—or even can't—share about a merger or acquisition. Keeping your cards close to your chest is imperative in ensuring business survival and growth. The lack of transparency when working on a merger or acquisition is unavoidable and often necessary in the merger and acquisition space. It is done knowingly to maintain shareholder/investor confidence, keep employees in key positions within the company from leaving, and to get through all of the legal and regulatory hoops required for a merger or acquisition to happen.

In addition to those reasons, the story for the "street" has to be carefully crafted, cultivated, and protected to ensure the transaction has the best possible chance for success. Your employees will experience this lack of short-term transparency as a form of deception. Entering into the deal-making space can be a mutable and ambiguous experience with many twists and turns along the way. Frankly, often executives and business owners don't know to what degree the level of fallout will be when engaged in a merger or acquisition. Although executives and business owners can plan and prepare for the deal, it is inevitable that there will always be changes that will need to be addressed and solutions incorporated along the way. As your dinner party planning progresses, the menu you serve may change.

Change in Economics

In 2008, the economic downturn showed us that in public and private companies alike, things can, and do, change very abruptly. At both Suncor and Petro-Canada, leadership had to start thinking about how they would maintain the viability of their organizations without spreading fear or panic. Rapid growth, skyrocketing costs, and an emerging war for qualified talent created the forecast for a perfect storm. There was a need to find a lifeline as key projects such as the development of the Fort Hills mine were being put on hold due to cost constraints.

In addition, the executive leadership of each company had to articulate the remedies they were prepared to use to mitigate the effects of the crisis to their shareholders. An example of leadership stepping in to provide assurance is an excerpt from Petro-Canada's 2008 Annual Report, *Strength to Deliver*. In that report, Petro-Canada's CEO answers questions about the economic downturn and the company's approach to managing though it: *"How has the downturn impacted Petro-Canada's suite of growth projects? We are pacing our growth projects through these challenging times to maintain growth in shareholder value. We intend to advance our three Board of Directors-approved projects as originally planned. […]we're waiting to see a recovery in commodity prices and financial markets before moving ahead. In the meantime, we're working to reduce project costs and execution risk."*

In Suncor's *2008 Annual Report*, the President and CEO's *Message to Shareholders*, told shareholders what Suncor would do to manage through the challenges ahead:

"In October, we reduced our 2009 capital spending plans to approximately $6 billion. But with no market correction in sight and to ensure we are living within our means, we visited this again in early 2009, reducing capital spending further to $3 billion. […]. As you can imagine, these were tough decisions to make. But difficult times demand we do what's right."

Each of these excerpts details the actions the respective CEOs planned to take to mitigate some of the fallout from the change in economics in their businesses. These communications were focused on shareholders, but employees also need to hear from the executives or owners of their company to help them understand the changes that may be afoot. They also need to be told what measures may need to be taken to manage the changes in economics, when appropriate. Regular communication to employees will help them deal with the uncertainty that a change in economics can bring.

Board Members and Executive Leadership Teams are in Town

Another key indicator that something big was about to happen was when I started seeing members of the executive leadership teams in the office more than normal. If your company is private, your employees may be seeing unfamiliar faces around with greater frequency. These folks could be potential buyers, accountants, or venture capitalists. It goes without saying that when big decisions need to be made, all of the key stakeholders need to be involved.

At Petro-Canada in late 2008 and early 2009, a lot of what was fueling the rumour mill was the number of executives and board members who were in town tied up in what appeared to be a lot of secret meetings. For most employees in the beginning, this was not of any particular significance, but as time progressed, and more people became involved in facilitating those meetings, it started to become more obvious that whatever the meetings were about, they most definitely had a higher degree of importance and secrecy. If your employees are seeing your executive leadership (Executive Vice President, Chief Financial Officer, General Counsel), Board Members, senior leaders (Vice President, General Managers, Directors), or owners in multiple meetings over a protracted period of time, they will likely surmise that an acquisition, divestiture, or change in the company is about to take place.

Rumours

In both public and private companies, it is not uncommon for rumours about the viability of the company to swirl around the office halls. There are always people within the organization and outside of it who speculate on what has happened, what is happening, and what will happen in the future. There are folks who are even paid to speculate on the future and the success of a given company. They are called Analysts and they make a living by providing speculative and/or research-based analysis of companies' economic health and wealth, and whether or not they look like a good investment for shareholders. Internally, these individuals typically work in departments such as Investor Relations, Corporate/Strategic Planning, or Accounting.

When there are rumours about the financial volatility of your company that are less than favourable, pay attention and address them with your employees! Long before the announcement of the merger between Suncor and Petro-Canada, the rumours internally were in full force. Rumours such as: were we going to acquire another company? If so, which company? Was the CEO going to retire? Externally for Suncor, the rumours sounded something like this:

"Last week, Suncor said it would cut its targeted spending for 2009 by a third to around $6 billion. [...]Despite the strong results, Suncor called the third quarter 'challenging,' saying unscheduled maintenance curbed production volumes. 'We're very well aware that we have disappointed the market in 2008. We're planning to rectify that here over the coming months,' [Suncor] told the conference call" (*Suncor defends oil sands as prices sag*, Globe and Mail October 30, 2008). Employees in both companies heard the rumours and had their own beliefs as to how things would be "rectified."

Work Slowdowns = Confusion

Petro-Canada and Suncor were thriving, growing, and buzzing with activity in 2008. Employees were focused on achieving their strategic goals and carrying out their business plans. In my first couple of years there, I felt a strong level of engagement and commitment to my work and the opportunities it afforded me. I felt great about my job and there was a legitimate sense of contentment in the projects I was working on and the possibilities ahead.

That vibe changed abruptly when the pace of business slowed down in early 2009. Work in some areas appeared to be motionless and eventually it became apparent that something was up. There were no new projects or work being sanctioned. There were no new hires and certain roles were not being replaced. Existing projects were delayed or put on hold, and, in some business units, people were enduring longer than normal periods of time where they were not busy. Management wasn't talking about more than the next couple of quarters when they discussed the business plan, and finally, the bench became long.

That means that for a time, there were more employees milling around certain areas of the company than there was available work to do, and I became concerned. Employees who are experiencing inertia in their day-to-day work for an extended period of time become demotivated, fearful, and are subject to confusion about their own work and capabilities as a result. It was a challenge to help leaders keep their remaining teams motivated when they themselves did not know what the next steps or outcome would be. My role during that uneasy time was to help leaders focus their teams on the work that they could do. This sometimes involved employees taking on projects outside of their direct accountabilities or working in a different area than they had been previously. Even some of my HR colleagues were moved out of roles supporting the oil sands business unit and joined other teams. In fact, a couple of them joined my team!

What I found most helpful during that time was knowing what each employee's skills and background were so that we could leverage them in ways we may not have previously. As HR professionals, executives, or business owners, we sometimes forget that an employee has specific experience or expertise in their history that they can use in a different setting. During any time of change or crisis, be it big or small, work-related or personal, understanding all of our own strengths and abilities is what will help get us through. Each of us needs to regularly fill up our own personal reservoir of talent, ability, and aptitudes so we can draw from it during a time of change.

As an executive or business owner, think of an employee's personal reservoir as a place containing experiences or personal strengths that have been used in the past to a positive effect. It was easy for me to think about my education, qualifications, and experience when I contemplated my work skills, but I also acquired specific life skills and capabilities along the way that I didn't view in the same light. Like many employees, I was a very focused, career-oriented person who was putting a lot of time and energy into my work. The slow-down in work triggered a different thinking process for me. I started to think about other dimensions outside of my work. How would I manage what was ahead? What could I add to top up my personal reservoir? Knowing what I know now, I would have focused on maintaining endurance and being mindful of how much of it I needed as changes occurred.

Layoffs

At Petro-Canada, we were all waiting to see what would happen next based on the rumours we heard. I personally assisted leaders with a number of layoffs in a key business unit and there was much consternation about the fact that it was happening. As an HR professional, I have been called on numerous times in my career to help leaders let go of their employees. Any Human Resources professional will tell you that the experience of terminating someone's employment is never easy—it's draining, and most unfortunate.

In the first few weeks of 2009, pre-merger, Petro-Canada was implementing ways to preserve cash to manage the change in economics. We found ourselves in the unenviable position of having to lay off a significant number of employees in the recently expanded oil sands business unit. During that time, I recall having a lot of empathy for one leader I worked with as we worked on a plan to dismantle the department he had staffed up to support the oil sands unit. It is hard to imagine what it would be like to build a strong team with great performers and within months have to find new jobs for them or plan for their terminations. I worked tirelessly with that leader to redeploy as many of his staff as we could. As termination day approached, I spent time assuring him that he did the best he could and that this was about the cost of doing business, not a personal failure on anyone's part. The humbleness and humanity he showed that day towards the employees he had to let go left an impression on him and me that I still reflect on today.

The task of terminating employees in these circumstances can be heartbreaking and unsettling. The employees and the leaders who are left behind after layoffs also feel unsettled and this feeling is not going to be abated for quite some time. The work groups that remain can spin into a form of lethargy that does not lend itself to high levels of confidence or productivity if not addressed regularly with care and concern for the morale of the employee base.

Stock Price

When a company is publicly traded and its stock price is perpetually undervalued, an executive team or Board will take actions to mitigate. Stock prices act as the temperature gauge of an organization's state of financial health. Although stock prices fluctuate, a stock price tends to serve as a lagging indicator of a company's wellbeing.

If the temperature of the organization is consistently below where it needs to be quarter after quarter, you can bet that the internal and external rumour mill will begin its churn. The economic crisis of 2008 subjected investors to increased volatility in their portfolios. Today's investors and analysts are constantly on

the look-out for quick returns and clear and consistent winners in terms of profit and value. Their portfolios have increasingly little room for shares that are continuously underperforming. Stock price is obviously important to employees because of the impact it can have on their own financial security. As an employee, I, too, had investments and a defined contribution pension that I wanted to grow and preserve. It was becoming a concern for me that our company's share price was not where it was expected to be.

Our world consists of defined contribution pension plans that rely on market-share performance and they can put an increasing burden on personal investments for our own and our family's wellbeing and long-term financial security. Most of us, regardless of our age or stage of career, are exposed to the vagaries of the market through our personal banking, pension plans, retirement savings, etc. Petro-Canada had been consistently undervalued in the marketplace and investor groups such as the Ontario Teacher's Pension Plan started to exert their influence in order to get Petro-Canada's Board and management to make changes to increase shareholder value.

The Ontario Teacher's Pension Plan is an independent organization responsible for administering defined-benefit pensions for school teachers of the Canadian province of Ontario. According to their website, they are the largest single-profession pension plan with $140.8 billion in net assets. Here is an excerpt from the February 6, 2009, *Globe and Mail* article by Andrew Willis detailing their effort at the time: *"The Ontario Teachers' Pension Plan stepped up the pressure on Petro-Canada yesterday in regulatory filings that showed the fund has dramatically increased its stake in the energy company, and it is pushing the board and management for improved performance. [...] Teachers also confirmed it has 'held discussions with the management and board of Petro-Canada regarding the creation of shareholder value. Those discussions are continuing.'"*

If your company is publicly traded and has a history of being undervalued in the market, the executive team and its Board will eventually need to take action to remedy that, whether it is initiated by them or not! In private companies, the economic rumblings look slightly different, but have an equally significant impact. The banks may no longer give the company money for capital and its cash flow may be reduced as a result. Vendors and suppliers will likely experience delays in payment and, in dire cases, there could be delay in making employee payroll or a need for staff cuts. These events will fuel rumours in the employee base and create cause for concern about the future of the company if not addressed quickly. Be as honest as possible about stock price and what some of the options to manage it might be.

Getting Your Guests Ready Before You Send the Invitation

Here are some simple and effective ways line-managers and supervisors can help employees ensure their reservoir levels are high enough to stay afloat during times of corporate uncertainty:

1. Encourage employees to stay flexible in their thinking and focused on the work at hand.

2. Suggest employees offer to assist other business units or departments that need help with projects.

3. Seek out continuous improvement opportunities for employees. When a work team is busy they may not have time to focus on improvements in process or procedures.

Something as simple as ensuring files and databases are accurate and up to date or cleaning up the workspace can help employees to refocus.

4. Encourage and position employees to participate in professional development activities to help them better manage through work slowdowns. If there are cost constraints or spending freezes, have employees refresh their employee resumes and professional profiles so they are up to date and reflect current skills or help others with theirs.

5. Create and promote ways for employees to stay consciously optimistic! Have regular one-on-one and team meetings with your employees. Allow time for employees to talk about their skill sets and where they see opportunities for improvements in the business. Ask them how they can help.

6. Support employees to show compassion for others who may be more anxious or concerned about the future than they are. Create opportunities for them to partner with each other on a project or key deliverable. Being of service to others shifts our focus and allows others to step up.

The point of sharing these rumblings is that when any one or combination of these events happen in your company, your employees' antennae will be raised and you need to communicate the news about what's happening in your organization as clearly and as openly as possible.

Here are some key points for a business owner or executive to consider when communicating to their preferred guests before inviting them to a grand dinner party. These key points are intended to help manage the rumblings in the transaction phase of the merger or acquisition. How well you manage those rumblings is an important indicator of the kind of invitation you will be sending your employees.

1. Highlight and clarify the type of dinner party you are having and why. Let your employees know what value each preferred guest brings that will add to the success of the party. During my own merger experience with Petro-Canada and Suncor, I recall being told we were merging, but in fact Petro-Canada was most definitely acquired.

The distinction between merging or acquiring, or takeover, is important when you are determining and communicating your dinner party theme and the strategy to your employee base. I didn't feel that the contributions my colleagues and I were bringing from Petro-Canada were going to be acknowledged or valued. Nor was it clear to us initially why we were being acquired by Suncor. The recognition of our different business cultures and what each would contribute to the vision was not clear to me and not validated by the executive leadership.

According to David Derain, Global Managing Director, Business Solutions at Hay Group, *"Culture is not an HR issue—it is a business issue. Business culture represents a class of assets which must be protected and properly aligned during the integration process if a merger is to succeed"* (Derain, D. 2007). The problem is that organizations don't clearly articulate the purpose of the merger or acquisition and the role that employees can or need to play to make it a success. This leaves employees asking why are these companies merging together, or why is this takeover necessary? You need to gain employees' trust by telling them the truth about why the merger or acquisition is happening.

So much time and effort is spent on the urgency to get the deal done and, as a result, there is not much appetite left for what is needed to make the vision come to life. Corporate vision, values, history, motivation, and the collective memories of each organization that drives them can be quite different.

It is incumbent upon the executives or business owners to understand what those differences are, examine and take inventory, and build a path forward that will properly and respectfully integrate the best parts to build a new and stronger company.

2. Determine what parts of the deal are compelling to your preferred guests. What menu items are you planning to offer them? A large-scale merger or acquisition can be a rewarding and enabling event that pushes an organization and its people toward increased sustainability and ultimately greater profitability than what existed before. Explain to employees what the opportunity is and how the new vision and strategy will position the new company to achieve it. Is the merger or acquisition about creating shared assets, spending available capital, gaining new technologies, or better market access?

3. Define what success looks like in the new company. A successful merger or acquisition is one where executives or business owners are able to bridge the excitement of the vision of the

new enterprise with expertise, experience, and engagement of employees tasked with the executing of that vision.

The business world today is complex, fast-paced, and changing relentlessly. As a human resources professional, I have seen how critically important it is for organizations to navigate their employees through the complexity of business transactions like mergers or acquisitions. It doesn't really matter if you are acquiring assets, people, or both. You need the heads, hearts, minds, commitment, and dedication of employees to make the deal work. Your dinner party theme will drive the execution of the transaction and ultimately its transformation.

Whenever a party is being planned there is usually a reason. Be it a celebration, or recognition, or the desire to come together to reconnect with others, there is always a reason to have a party. As an executive or business owner, you need to be conscious in articulating what the company and its employees will gain. Those gains could be obvious based on the rumblings that have been occurring. If your company is combating low share price, layoffs, or cash flow issues, the gain could be that you will have more stability, better market position, increased cash flow or better technology and processes.

As an executive team or business owner contemplates the corporate vision, they need to balance that vision with the realities of today. Providing context to the rumblings within the long-term aspiration for the company is complex but necessary. Executives and business owners in today's business world are extremely focused on the transaction part of making a deal happen and that's a good thing. During the transaction phase of the merger or acquisition, however, it is very important to communicate your dinner party theme or vision.

A vision can't be so grand that it makes your guests feel that they can't buy into it. Vision is much like the envelope for your invitation. What is contained inside that envelope needs to be carefully planned for so your guests can understand what's to come at the party and where the company is going and start to think about how they can contribute to its success. In the next chapter we will delve further into the importance of having corporate values and crafting the right invitation for your preferred guests.

"Be clear on your vision and strategy. Know why you're doing it and be specific about what you gain."

– Donna Garbutt, CEO, Maxxam Analytics

"You're most vulnerable immediately at the time of the announcement, it's really important and, frankly, if you're an organization that's growing by acquisition, you should be out there all of the time talking about what you believe in."

– Margot Micallef, QC, President, Oliver Capital Partners

Key Insights

Vision

- Declare your corporate vision early. Vision is the theme of the party you are inviting your employees to.

- Share what you are doing and why, when you are able to do so. Give your guests confidence by being transparent so they understand what's happening and can get excited about what's ahead.

- Determine who should be invited to the table and why. Communicate the value of your guests and the company they came from, and how they can contribute to the vision.

CHAPTER 3

Who's Coming for Dinner?

Craft The Invitation and Your Company's Values

As executives and business owners consider a merger or acquisition, they should be seriously contemplating what values are wanted and needed to move the organization's vision and strategy forward. One of the first ways is by carefully preparing, planning for, and researching the acquisitions they choose in order to make the right deal. Researching and inviting the right preferred guests to the table as well as ensuring the guests know why they are there and what role they are to play is like feeding them a fantastic menu that includes a tasty value proposition, which is key to a successful merger or acquisition. The second and most important way executives and business owners can make an impact is to be unequivocal about the values they want to have in the new organization.

Culture and the values that underpin it should be viewed as a consciousness shared amongst many. Culture is fluid and it resonates with people over time as they share common points of reference and experience. Much like planning for your dinner party, deciding what your culture is going to be early is essential. Knowing what the merger or acquisition is supposed to achieve and being clear on the outcomes is important because it is a key predictive indicator of the kind of culture the organization will develop over time. The values that will support that culture are even more important because they will determine who will be a part of the organization and *how* the organization will run. Simply put, culture can be defined as *values in action*.

Identify and Invite Preferred Guests

When you are planning a successful dinner party, time and consideration must be taken to create the ideal guest list. Having a clear and detailed understanding of whom you are going to invite is necessary and the most significant part of the planning. When building your guest list, speed can be good, but thoughtful consideration of which guests should attend and the mix of guests is better! Once the news of a merger or acquisition or any significant change is finally made public, it is incumbent upon a business owner or executive to quickly address a number of key issues that impact employees.

If these issues are not acknowledged and managed properly, the event will be off to a rocky start and mistrust in the employee ranks will quickly take root. After declaring the vision, the next most critical issue to address is determining the company's core values so employees can decide if they want to be a part of the new company or not. An appealing invitation that speaks to the values of the new company will bring employees to the table excited and anticipating what's next.

Deciding Who's Coming for Dinner

During the Suncor/Petro-Canada merger, we were told the two organizations were quite similar in terms of culture and ways of doing business. That, of course, was not exactly true, but it was the perspective of the executive team who had vested interests in making the deal happen. Executives and business owners alike need to do their homework on any acquisition they intend to make. Many organizations rely solely on what the executive team or investors say about their respective company, its employees, culture, values, and ways of achieving its goals. Preferred guests are the employees or key stakeholders internal or external to your merged or acquired company. The wrong mix of preferred guests at your dinner party will certainly cost you more in the end. Some questions to help you determine which guests should be invited are:

1. How do these preferred guests think?

2. What value will they contribute to your dinner party/company?

3. How many guests need to be invited and when?

4. Do the guests align with the corporate values and culture?

Most importantly, get under the hood of the company you are acquiring or merging with, and find out how the employees or "preferred guests" operate. Don't be in a hurry to exclude people from your guest list in a race to create synergy! Some invitees will RSVP and decide to come to the dinner, and others will decide they don't want to stay over time. Take the appropriate amount of time to craft your corporate values and the employee invitation. If you hurry, your party will be jeopardized and more expensive, or you will need to have several costly dinner parties (mergers/acquisitions) to ensure you are getting the right mix of employees and preferred guests. Executives and business owners can start to build engagement by determining what values are required in the new company. The following are some questions to consider as you contemplate the values of your new merged/acquired company.

Which Values Will Drive Performance?

If collaboration is deemed to be an important value to drive company performance, describing how that looks in the new company is critical. A business owner or executive needs to take time to understand how both legacy organizations interpret and describe what collaboration means. In one company, collaboration might mean working cross-functionally across departments on large projects. In the other company, it could be interpreted as getting consensus on every decision and slowing down business decision-making to ensure consensus is achieved.

The risk of not defining this value in the context of how it drives performance is that your guests, internal and external, will be confused. Collaboration should facilitate and support key processes, systems, and workflows in the new company. In a company where there is a high level of integration, collaboration as a value will attract the right guests who are able to work in that type of environment. As you map out the new company's processes and systems, the value of collaboration and how it will be incorporated into those processes and systems needs to be identified and defined.

What Behaviours Will Be Rewarded to Ingrain the Values and Culture?

If we use the example of integrity as a value, what does integrity actually look like in the new company? What happens if there are problems or defects with your product or the services you provide to your customers? What actions will the company take? If integrity is a corporate value, the organization will do what's needed to make it right. This could include refunding a customer or changing a production process to ensure better quality over time.

These actions let employees know what the company stands for and reaffirms the values it wants to uphold. To illustrate how values can guide an organization's way of doing business, here are some scenarios that demonstrate corporate values in action.

Integrity

The newly merged company has chosen integrity as one of its core values. As one of the outcomes of the recent merger, there will be employee layoffs to contain costs and reduce duplication in the workforce. This means that 30% of the combined workforce will lose their jobs. While the employee terminations are happening, the ten-member executive team decides to go on a weeklong off-site at a five-star resort in Florida to plan the future direction and strategy of the company. Employees will question why cost-cutting does not apply to those executives. Living the values by demonstrating the behaviour is crucial in establishing and embedding the value. The executives needed to discuss the direction of the new company but did they need to do that at an expensive resort out of town? What message does that send to the employees? What happens to executives and employees if they choose not to act with integrity but get business results anyway?

The consequence of not living a corporate value consistently will result in a lack of employee trust. The climate and culture of the organization is set by the executives or business owner. Be mindful of how the values are demonstrated in action and the visibility of those actions to employees.

Which of the Preferred Guests Will Be Championing the Values?

Know who the key players are at *each* level of the organization and work to engage them in the pre-transformation process right away. These key players not only translate the corporate vision to their teams, they are also the folks who will embed the values and shape the culture of the organization in its earliest stages. Intentionally select champions such as line-level managers, supervisors, and top-performing employees. They should be rewarded for being examples of committed and relentless champions of the new corporate values.

Respect

Jim is getting great results every quarter in sales, but it is known that there have been complaints from colleagues on the team about him making racist and sexist remarks in team meetings and in one-on-one interactions. Mel, a new employee joining the team, observes Jim making inappropriate comments to a female colleague and is shocked. He makes a complaint to their manager, Joe. Joe has been made aware of these types of inappropriate comments before and has raised the issue with Jim. Jim stops for a while but then reverts to being offensive and inappropriate within a few days. Joe decides this time that he will escalate the complaint to their Director of Sales because he doesn't see Jim demonstrating the corporate value of respect. When Joe raises this with Kathy, their Director of Sales, she agrees the behaviour is inappropriate but indicates that Jim exceeds his sales targets consistently every quarter and has brought in a lot of new customers and added revenue in the last three years. She has given him bonuses for exceeding targets this year when sales have dropped off by 20 percent due to a slow market. She tells Joe to tell Mel that she will take his complaint to HR even though she will not do so for fear of losing a very good, revenue-generating sales person. As a senior leader in the organization, Kathy's behaviour is a visible representation of the real values of the organization and respect is not one of them.

Community

What will the new company's expression of values be in the communities in which it operates? How would your customers and peer companies describe how your company does business?

59

A community can include the industry the company is part of or the city or town in which it operates. How is the organization viewed by the outside world? Are the values consistently applied internally and externally?

Safety

Company J is a small energy company that produces natural gas. It has a gas plant located a few miles outside of a small farming community. One of their core values is safety. Maria is a Health and Safety Advisor and over the years has taken pride in the fact that she works for a company that places a high focus on the safety of its operations and its workers. When an unexpected, minor gas leak occurs at one of Company J's facilities, she is surprised to learn that there will be no internal investigation or debriefing of the leak, and the employees involved have been told to keep quiet as it is a minor incident. Eventually, news of the incident hits the local newspaper and when she is at a family dinner a few days later she is asked about what happened because of her health-and-safety background. Maria is uncomfortable and cannot explain how Company J is handling this safety matter. The fact that the leadership team has not explained what happened or what to do to prevent it from happening again is confusing and Maria doesn't feel equipped to address this with people in her community. It leaves her and her family wondering if Company J truly does value safety.

Values Are the Company's DNA

Crafting the invitation in the merger or acquisition context is about declaring the new company's values. Those values need to resonate so they can be integrated and articulated by all employees. Values are the company's DNA. They represent what a company is, what it stands for, and how it does business. Ensuring the employees you are inviting to your dinner party align to your vision and values is extremely important as you begin the merger journey. Why? It gives a clear line of sight to where the new company is going and how they will operate. It enables employees to decide if they want to be a part of the company or not. Most importantly, it shows that leadership is accountable to uphold and steward the values. Alignment of values with the corporate vision will create the foundation of the new organization going forward.

We have all been to a dinner where the evening was an engaging exchange of ideas, food, and camaraderie. Some of us have also been to a dinner party where we couldn't wait to leave as we had nothing in common with the other guests or the host didn't welcome us in the way that we would have liked. If we remember that the executive mindset should be one of invitation, creating an invitation that is appealing and details how the company will operate needs to be at the beginning of the transaction phase of the merger or acquisition. Who executives and business owners invite to the dinner party is a key step in laying the foundation for merger success.

"It's important to communicate the value system because that's how you determine whether or not people belong within that organization. It is about engagement, which is fundamental for success."

– Margot Micallef, QC, President, Oliver Capital Partners

"Are you living the values you have declared? And if you're not, there are two simple solutions: 1) change your values or 2) change your behaviour, but you have to have the tone where what you say is what you do."

– Heather Eddy, MSc., Senior HR Consultant

Key Insights

Values

- Corporate vision is aspirational. Values are experiential. Values are how employees experience working in a company. Create an invitation that employees are excited to accept.

- Values are the company's DNA. They are the core of what a company is, what it stands for, how it treats it employees, and how it does business.

- Trust is built by how consistently and visibly corporate values are lived.

PRE-TRANSFORMATION

CHAPTER 4

Welcome Your Guests

Be a Good Host: Develop an On-Boarding Plan

On-board Your Newly Acquired Employees

Pre-transformation is the phase where the integration of the merged or acquired company begins. This is where the hard work of understanding how each company operates and creating a plan to put together a newer, larger entity takes place. It is also where the employees from both companies will begin to work together.

Imagine being invited to a dinner party by some new neighbours who recently moved onto the same street. You and your spouse accept the invitation and look forward to meeting and welcoming them to the neighbourhood. They, too, have young children similar in age to your own and maybe they can play together. You arrive at their house at 6:00 pm per the invitation, and are greeted at the door by them. After serving you some punch, they proceed to visit and mingle amongst their friends from their old neighbourhood and leave you and your spouse sitting on the deck by yourselves. You both attempt to introduce yourselves to the other guests and to strike up conversation, but, while polite, they continue to talk about a story of a trip they all went on ten years ago and ignore you for most of the evening. After dessert is served, you leave the party right away and wonder why you were invited.

This example speaks to the importance of first impressions and orienting people to new situations. The hosts were keen to include their new neighbours in their home. They didn't, however, take the time to welcome them and orient them to their existing community of friends or their house! The same applies in a corporate setting. The intention is to include the new employees, but executives and business owners don't have a plan to fulfill that intention, and therein lies the problem. The first impression you make on your newly acquired employees, and *how* you make that impression, will set the tone going forward. If you do not orient and on-board your new and existing employees to the ways of the new company quickly and with purpose, a lack of commitment, trust, and ultimately loss of productively will result. When bringing employees into the merged organization, leaders at all levels need to be their hosts.

On-boarding, in simple terms, means welcoming your employees. If part of your acquisition plan is to retain talent as well as assets, it is important to make your newly acquired employees feel welcome in the new organization. Remember to reach out to the existing ones too! On-board both new and existing employees with as much care and attention as you would a brand-new hire into your new company. Why is this important? The company that the existing employees worked for yesterday will not look the same post-merger or acquisition.

Fear *will* creep into the employee ranks when the future is unknown and the connection to the history of the old company is lost. Recognizing and stemming the fears of employees going through large-scale business changes is important. It ensures the new company retains enough of the right employees and aligns them to the future vision and the urgent business tasks at hand for integration. It's also an opportunity for the new owners and/or executives to market the new vision and brand of the newly merged or acquired company. Think of it as welcoming your guests to the dinner party and showing them the new house they will work in and guiding them to the table where they will be seated. Your guests shouldn't have to try to find the dinner table. Be a good host.

In my own merger experience, I remember the feeling of being nervous about the future and yet cautiously optimistic at the same time. I wanted to understand how things would work in the new company and, more importantly, what my place was. We were expected to work in the new company helping to integrate work teams and yet didn't know what our own fate was. From the period of March 23, 2009, until October 2009, I didn't actually know if I would continue to have a job. The HR team I worked with also did not know they had jobs until the last weeks of the initial merger transaction process.

The transition for employees going through a merger or

acquisition can be a difficult one. Employees will become fearful because they don't know what to expect. As a host, you want to create a relationship with your guests. This establishes a foundation of trust and creates buy-in early. If the relationship is not set up correctly, fear will set in. Understanding and addressing the fear is an important first step in the on-boarding process.

Fear – Loss and Lost

The fear of failure and the fear of success stem from the same place. Whether we succeed or fail, we fear that which we will lose.

Fear is a double-edged emotion. It is one of our most basic and innate responses. It protects us by pushing us to flee from danger or to confront that danger. In either case, it is a visceral and immediate response to that which is in front of us. The rumblings have now confirmed your employees' suspicions. Your company is merging, being acquired, or being taken over by another company. Or, your company is the one taking over another company and acquiring their people and their assets to boost the balance sheet.

Whatever the case, you can guarantee that a change is going to happen and your employees will be working in a different corporate landscape. Think of an apple cart as a familiar metaphor. For many employees, a merger or acquisition will represent a much-needed shift, providing opportunities for personal and professional growth, so they will be adding apples to their cart. For others, their apple cart will be knocked over and this will initially cause apprehension and result in emotional and mental numbness for a time.

Imagine the cart holds many apples and they represent

significant professional elements that comprise a person's corporate identity and persona. For example, one apple represents a person's confidence (their knowledge and experience gained in their current position), another signifies the person's ego (personal and professional identity) and yet another represents relationships (with co-workers and others, developed on a professional level). As employees witness their apple cart tumbling over, it is very emotional. All of those important professional attributes gained are now dropping out of the cart and onto the ground.

As employees retrieve the apples to place them back into their apple carts, they will discover that some may have become bruised and others may have temporarily lost their lustre and shine, while others appear to not be scathed at all. The fear that welled up within me when my apple cart was upset was not so much about the fear of the unknown that was yet to unfold, it was about what I was going to lose. Losing the job that I enjoyed and interesting work that challenged me and got me jumping out of bed in the morning was part of that fear. Losing the camaraderie and professional relationships with colleagues that I had nurtured—something that I cherished— added to that fear. Losing connection and footing with what I had known and come to take for granted was an unnerving disruption. This initial fear can also permeate at home with family and friends. As I ruminate on that time, I am brought right back to that place where that sense of fear still feels fresh. Your employees may be grappling with some of these fears as well. Here are some of the apples that fell out of my apple cart:

Confidence – Will You Like Me Once You Know Me?

In the beginning of any relationship, whether personal or professional, first impressions are lasting impressions. I remember feeling excited and nervous about the new combined leadership team in human resources. The team was made up of managers and directors from both Petro-Canada and Suncor. The mix of leaders was fairly evenly split, with more Petro-Canada managers to start with in the beginning.

Although some of these folks would eventually move on, I was curious to know if some of these leaders—some old and some new—would truly understand my talents and capabilities and those of my colleagues. What was going to happen to the work I was doing and how would this change impact my career in the

reported to, whereas ours were not. As we hunkered down into the employee relations work stream, I often felt like I was secretly being interviewed. This wasn't actually the case, but as I met new counterparts from Suncor and engaged with them to start the integration process, I couldn't escape the feeling of wanting and needing to prove myself to the new group of leaders. I suppose I felt that way because I wasn't sure they would see my value and wasn't quite sure who was watching and who was assessing my skills and capabilities. I had an anxious energy during that time.

Your employees' professional identities, accomplishments, and what kind of workers they are will be on display again much like it is when they start a new job at a new company. The difference in this scenario is they are bringing with them all of their resident knowledge and, at times, some residue of their last experience. They want to show up to the dinner party dressed and ready for the event! As an employee, it was my view that it's up to employees to re-prove/improve their worth to accomplish their own goals, especially if their manager or supervisor is no longer with the company. As a business owner or executive, you need to provide opportunities for employees to show what they can do during a disruptive time. During this time, pay more attention to them and treat them like the most important guests at the table.

Relationships

So much of employees' satisfaction in their daily work is derived from the relationships they have with their colleagues and friends. When a merger or acquisition takes place, one of the apples that gets tossed out of the cart is relationships. The prospect of losing our connection to our work group, co-workers, trusted leaders, or friends is a very difficult one. The sense of trust and shared values is challenged as people leave the company or groups are split apart due to reorganization in the company.

Just as I was beginning to feel I had earned the trust of my peers and leaders, the workplace changed. I enjoyed the camaraderie, friendships, and fun that we had. We had many shared experiences that connected us, and that was going to change. Would that all disappear after the dust settled? Who would stay and who would go? Was the new workplace going to be as welcoming and enjoyable? The idea of leaving that behind was by far one of the most difficult parts of the merger for me to accept because it had been a satisfying environment for me to work in. I felt part of something bigger.

We can all think of a time when a co-worker has left to join a new company. We say we will keep in touch as we wish them the best in their new role. The reality is that once they are gone, we rarely maintain the same connection to that person because they have exited our physical and mental space. As time passes, your employees will develop new and different relationships, but losing connections with existing colleagues will happen and be tough. In some cases, they will leave great relationships with their co-workers and friends behind. Be aware that relationships are a key motivator for employees and the loss of relationships will impact them for some time.

Bruised Ego

My definition of a bruised ego is when employees with high levels of skill, ability, and performance can't utilize any of that energy to contribute to the newly emerging entity. The ego is bruised because there is chasm between the memory of being efficient and productive and the reality that those skills may no longer be needed, wanted, or acknowledged.

The employee and the ego are caught in an uncomfortable position. They want people to know that they know something and to be heard. My experience is that employees want to make their best contribution, and when faced with the task of integration or any business challenge, most will want to bring their best thinking and abilities to their new employer to help make the company successful. This help may or may not be well received or welcomed.

This was a realization I eventually had but it wasn't immediately evident. During the process of a corporate merger or acquisition, there will be winners and losers. It sounds trite, but the process of deciding who will stay and who will not *will* happen. In some cases, executives and business owners will have an idea of what employee skill sets they need and who has them. In other cases, they may not have a clear idea and will see which employees fit best where over time. This typically happens within the first 12 months of a merger or acquisition, although it can take longer. As time passed and integration activities progressed, I surmised that the talents and capabilities that had made some employees successful no longer fit in the new wilderness the merger created. Like the sun rising over an icy, cold tundra, the realization is subtle, distant, and it's rays faint.

Over time, I felt I was not as effective as I once was. I was still the same person, with the same level of education, expertise, and work experience, but somehow I didn't fit in the same way. Why doesn't my apple shine like it used to? At times I questioned my own competence and abilities as the merger lagged on. I felt disconnected and my ego for a time was bruised. The feeling of having a bruised ego will come and go over the course of time as employees hit different patches in the road, and it is a normal reaction to have. It is important to recognize that there is a tension created between leveraging resident knowledge and managing resistance to change. How that tension is managed will eventually determine your employees' ability and desire to stay with the new organization.

The reason I have shared my own experience in this much detail is that I believe leaders within organizations, as well as the executives or business owners, are not always close enough to the day-to-day activities of their employees. In my merger experience, I didn't feel like leadership at any level understood or cared about my involvement. Coupled with the lack of clarity about my job security, it was an area in which I believe the organization and many like it could do better. As a HR professional, business owner, or executive, here are three simple steps that will alleviate employee fear, build trust, and on-board your employees effectively.

P.A.S. – Plan, Acknowledge, and Share

These are the three key levers executives or business owners can use to quickly orient and on-board employees during the initial first few days and weeks of the integration phase of a merger or acquisition.

Plan – Showing Your Guests the Way by Welcoming Them

The Plan is focused on orienting employees to the new company and providing them with the basics to equip them to start the integration work ahead. Orientation is when you show your guests your home and where to find things. It's the first step in on-boarding your employees. The plan outlines what employees need to know to start in the new company and, more importantly, how to be successful in the new company.

For example, what are the things they will need to know in the first week after the company has merged or been acquired? The first two weeks? The first 30 days? Where is the new office? How can employees get access to email, parking, benefits, and the other basic details most workers will need to get started? Orient these new guests to the party. Show your employees how things work in the new organization. Demonstrating that you have thought through these details will inspire confidence and good will amongst employees. Many companies have checklists to help leaders orient new employees to the company. This orientation step becomes even more critical in a merger or acquisition. Below is a sample orientation checklist that highlights some basic orientation steps. It is by no means exhaustive, but it gives you an idea of what's important in welcoming your employees.

On-Boarding Checklist

Laying out a plan for employees to orient themselves during a time of upheaval will help them to be productive quickly. Remind them why they are part of the new organization and explain how they can contribute. Introduce them and partner them with the other guests. Let them know why they were invited to the dinner party. Even better, let them tell you how they think they can contribute or why they should continue to be preferred guests!

☐ *Senior leaders greet employees by their name. "We heard you were coming, we've been waiting for you to arrive, and we are looking forward to working with you." Let employees know they matter and why they are important.*

☐ *Introduce employees to their co-workers and colleagues. This is especially important if the work team is mixed with employees from both companies.*

☐ *Pair a new employee with an existing employee. This is someone that they will partner with over the next 30-60 days to learn how things get done in the new company.*

☐ *Hold an information session for employees of both organizations.*

☐ *Show employees their work space and where the printer, supplies, etc. are located.*

☐ *Review workplace policies and procedures and health and safety information.*

☐ *Review workplace expectations, including key work deliverables and the process of how progress on those deliverables will be measured.*

Within 60 days, employees should know what their work plans/ responsibilities are in detail and be partnered with their merger peers and line-supervisor to start creating the new organization. Within 90 days, they should have a clear idea of what goals and outcomes they will be measured against and line-leaders should be checking in on their employees' progress. In addition, those line-leaders need to provide feedback, encouragement, and guidance to ensure there is alignment with the goals and direction of the new company. By focusing on shared goals, you start to build the team's sense of shared accountability and their sense of community.

Acknowledge - Building a Sense of Belonging with Your Employees

"[…] *when you honor your past, you start to see the myriad of ways that your skills and experiences can serve you.*"

– Gail Blanke, Between Trapezes (2004)

People want to belong. Creating a sense of belonging within your employee base sets the foundation for engagement. What does belonging in the post-merger context mean? When employees are engaged, they are able to focus freely on helping rebuild the new company and pursue its goals. Highly sought-after outcomes like reliability, predictability, and stability in the newly merged or acquired entity are contingent on external factors such as commodity pricing, market share, stock price, etc. Internally—and equally as important—is employee engagement.

The probability of the new company's success is directly proportionate to an executive's or business owner's ability to create a community for employees. Without engagement there is no belonging, and without belonging there isn't a sense of community. A strategic lever in creating a sense of community is acknowledgement. Acknowledgement is a powerful thing. When you acknowledge your employees and their contributions, you are helping them decide how to feel about the merger. You have the opportunity to influence their view of what will happen next. As human beings, we have an innate need to be acknowledged and to belong. When you notice and appreciate the effort and contribution of your employees, and you embed a culture of acknowledgement, people begin to connect—not just to each other, but to the vision the organization is trying to create.

The best dinner parties are those that include the shared stories and experiences of all the invited guests. New friendships and memories are often created at these gatherings. The same can hold true for a merged or acquired organization. It can start with something as simple as appreciating each other's differences within both companies, and the collective past(s) of each legacy organization, or acknowledging that each employee brings a set of skills and capabilities that can be used to further the goals of the workgroup or business unit. It is easy to overlook this point, as there are often many tasks to focus on.

Engagement, by definition, is an obligation or agreement to do something. When employees are engaged, they are more than willing to expend the necessary discretionary effort to create success in the newly merged organization. Any good change management model will specifically articulate the importance of communication. Communicate, communicate, and then communicate some more. Employees who are experiencing a merger will always focus on self-preservation. Instead of allowing that to be an obstacle, acknowledge it and promote an environment of authenticity.

Allow your preferred guests to express their fears and channel those emotions by letting them tell you how they can make a difference in the new organization. Not only will you open the channel for change, but you will also begin to embed a sense of personal accountability for success. It is important to remember that the people doing the tasks are the most vital part of making a merger work, not the tasks themselves. Ensuring your guests feel welcome and engaged creates excitement for what's next and goes a long way to creating an enjoyable party.

Share – Engaging to Create Outcomes and Community

At this stage, it should be clear to your employees why they are here and what they are here to accomplish. The pre-transformation phase of the merger is focused on defining and implementing the way forward and will require employees on both sides of the merger or acquisition to adopt the new way of doing business. For some employees, that new way will be the existing way they are used to doing things and for others it will be a time of significant change. In either case, the success of the merger or acquisition itself is dependent on your employees having a clear understanding of what the new company is about, and how they can contribute to its success.

Leaders need to create opportunities for employees to get to know each other. Like any good dinner party, when the guests have the opportunity to interact over the course of the evening, it builds comfort, interest, and anticipation for what's next. Allow your line-leaders the time to create opportunities for employees to share. Share time with each other, share experiences with one another, and share ideas and best practices. Getting to know your new colleagues and teams is not a new idea. It is, however, one that is overlooked or downplayed during a time of significant change. In my experience, the more employees know about you and each other on a personal level, the more willing they are to work with each other as a team. The most effective teams I had as a leader were those where the team were connected and appreciated each other and were willing to help one another in the work based on that connection.

Irrespective of how much or little fear your employees experience after the merger or acquisition, it is important to remember that they have so much to offer. The fear of what will happen next will be present for them in some form or another and it will come and go. Even though fear and doubt immobilized me for a short time, I was eventually comforted by exciting possibilities ahead and a vision of hope that new and good things were to come. When you think about what's next for you and your employees as the changes unfold, ask yourself: are you really ready? Do you understand what concerns your employees have? Do you have a plan to orient them to the new vision and values? Have you thought about how you will get employees, both newly acquired and existing, to work together effectively?

A thoughtful on-boarding plan for all employees regardless of which company they come from or how long they have been with their respective organizations is important because it lets employees know that they are welcome in the new company. Welcoming employees helps them understand what the new company is about and is one of the first ways that the new company shows its employees what the value proposition is. Acknowledging the past and employees' contributions from both companies opens the door to engagement and future collaboration. It helps dilute the "us against them" mentality that can occur after a merger or acquisition.

Encouraging employees to share who they are and what's important to them creates a feeling of belonging within a team. These three steps are important in building an engaged and able workforce. Most importantly, they also enable the new leadership team to start laying the foundation of trust, which is essential as the newly merged or acquired organization progresses into pre-transformation—the most challenging phase.

"Through the merger and restructuring, we wanted to make sure that we didn't lose people, so we focused on communication, helping them see the vision for the new organization. It is almost best to over-communicate to help give people clarity in order to motivate them to stay and see what role they may have in the new organization."

– Perry Schuldhaus, President, Enbridge Income Fund Holdings Inc. (ENF)

Key Insights

- Be a good host. Welcome and on-board your employees to your dinner party. Create excitement by letting them know why they are there.

- Employees will be emotional and experience degrees of fearfulness. Build trust by creating a detailed change plan to get them up to speed quickly.

CHAPTER 5

Setting the Table

Prepare for Employee Engagement

In Latin, the word *fides* is defined as a promise, assurance, word of honor, or engagement. In the post-merger or acquisition aftermath, the way you set your table will indicate to your guests what you are about to serve. It indicates the promise of what is yet to come. This is where the value proposition of the merger or acquisition comes to life or dies.

As an executive, business owner, or host of this party, you will need to have a plan to engage those whom you have invited to ensure their hard work brings the most value during pre-transformation. A robust and meaningful pre-transformation or change plan will ensure that you are acting as an attentive host with employees as you embark on making changes ahead. The problem that many leadership teams face when merging is that they have not created a strategy for transformation. There isn't a clear plan on how to engage employees in the pre-transformation phase of a merger or acquisition.

Getting the utensils and the place setting right isn't always considered during a merger or acquisition. This gap in planning pre-empts any possibility of a successful merger or acquisition, and will cause expensive delays. If you are serving soup, you will want to ensure you have spoons and not forks! How the table is set, where your guests will sit, and what utensils are laid out tell your guests what to expect. It provides clues on what will be served and how.

The table may be set with fancy silver cutlery, china, ornate napkins and decorations, or very simply with everyday dishes and placemats. The table setting is the first time your employees are going to see how you intend to do business going forward. Pre-transformation begs the following questions: what people, processes, and technology will be required for the new company to run? Executives and business owners need to ask themselves if they have the right utensils on the table of their dinner party to move forward successfully with the merger or acquisition. Setting the table is where the theme and the invitation of the party or *fides* come to life, and where the promise of what's to come is unveiled. The work that comes before the new organization's transformation is critical to a merger or acquisition's success and, trust me, it takes a lot of hard work.

Setting the Table Prepares for Engagement

Setting the table is without question the most important step before preparing to serve a meal to your guests. It's so critical that it is the sub-title of this book. Can you imagine having a dinner party and not having plates or cutlery to eat the food with? Can you imagine inviting your friends, family, and acquaintances to a meal at your home and then waiting until they arrive to decide what to serve them? Or worse, making them wait while you decide how to make the meal you want to serve them? Strangely enough, in mergers or acquisitions, there is often no plan that outlines what tools, processes, goals, or outcomes the employees should get ready to engage in and be a part of. Executives and business owners don't always consider the need to have a plan for pre-transformation.

That plan should clearly outline how things are intended to go and the path to get there. Let's take a look at how a place setting is very much like preparing employees for the new company's transformation.

1. Utensils are the organization's technology. They enable processes that get the food—the company's business outcomes—to the plate.

2. Plates hold the processes and the technology works with what's on the plate.

3. The meal about to be served is the new company's value proposition coming to life.

The people, processes, and technology that will be required to move the transaction forward need to be not only contemplated but designed as much as possible in order for the deal to work. How to address these will be described in more detail in the *Building Your Pre-Transformation Plan* section of this chapter. Once you have started the merger or acquisition process with another organization and know who your preferred guests will be, it will be absolutely essential to determine which company will be responsible for leading the way. That means one company, in some way, shape, or form will take one for the team.

Someone Will Take One for The Team

By the summer of 2009, I was ready and raring to go as Suncor and Petro-Canada began to create plans for their integration. The apples in my cart were a bit bruised, but I was keen to see how I could contribute to the merging of these companies. I was going to shine the apples up again by engaging in some really interesting integration work. What a great experience to add to my portfolio! We were going to merge! We had some good stuff and so did Suncor, so if we put it together it would be really great, right? Well, not exactly.

In the case of Petro-Canada and Suncor, the merger was seen as a marriage of equals by the marketplace. In terms of company size and number of employees, this was true. As the process of integration unfolded, this was not the case. Employees were told many times by the leadership teams of both companies that we were merging the two companies together and that the transaction was a merger of equals: *"Mergers are rarely a marriage of equals, and it's still the case that most acquirers or dominant merger partners pursue a strategy of cultural absorption; the acquired company or smaller merger partner is expected to assimilate and adopt the culture of the other. Whether the outcome is successful depends on the willingness of organizational members to surrender their own culture, and at the same time perceive that the other culture is attractive and therefore worth adopting"* (Cartwright, 2015).

There was an abrupt recognition on the part of Petro-Canada employees that we were not told the whole story. What came to light very early on in the integration process was very different. In fact, Petro-Canada was taken over by Suncor and the act of absorption began. It was like we came to the dinner party prepared for a four-course dinner and found out that the dinner table was set for a barbeque! My memory of that time is of being completely gripped by the culture of Suncor. The vestiges of Petro-Canada were to be done away with in key areas such as people, processes, and technology, and that resulted in a feeling of being betrayed by leadership on both sides of the deal. Wasn't this supposed to be a merger of equals? This was a surprisingly hard pill to swallow in the beginning. To be honest, we weren't given enough water (support) to knock that pill back initially. Petro-Canada, in fact, was going to become a part of Suncor, lock, stock, and cash on the barrelhead. We were becoming Suncor, not merging with it! What was Petro supposed to gain from this transaction? We were the company that did the acquiring, not the other way around.

"For shareholders over in the Petro-Canada corner, there is relief, even if it is coloured with a tinge of resentment. 'The merger doesn't do anything for Petro-Canada,' said one former Petro-Canada shareholder" (Tait, 2009). I, too, like many internal and external Petro-Canada stakeholders, questioned the merger and what the real benefits were going to be. That being said, the reason that this merger has not failed is because Petro-Canada decided to take one for the team by surrendering its culture, accomplishments, and autonomy to become part of Suncor. Employees read what the analysts were reporting as to why the merger was happening, but unfortunately employees didn't hear it stated enough by our own leadership at the time.

One company's way of doing business will need to be the preferred way as you begin the pre-transformation process. This is important because if one way of doing business is not declared up front, you run the risk of having multiple systems and processes which become very costly. You also run the risk of inadvertently creating an "us against them" mentality within the various group of employees and/or other stakeholders. What key  processes, workflows, or outputs should the newly created organization use to start with? These may change as the business of the company evolves, but, without question, one way needs to be declared early and clearly to start aligning employees.

Just like setting the table for your dinner party, preparing employees for pre-transformation lets them know what to expect and what integration activities will be focused on. To be clear, in a merged or acquired entity there is no such thing as equality. Someone will always take one for the team. If not, the act of integration or absorption will not proceed effectively and the merger transaction will have limited possibilities for long-standing success.

The richness of a corporate vision going forward and the richness of shared history should be acknowledged and combined in order to move the organization forward, but this is not easy to do. In the case of a merger or acquisition, one organization, or sometimes both, have to sacrifice certain things to enable future success. Mergers or acquisitions can be an arduous undertaking and the vision of two organizations coming together seamlessly to create something better is more easily envisioned than enacted.

In my research for this book, when I interviewed people who have been through mergers or acquisitions, all of them without exception shared their view that the merger equation is not one with equal parts, and employees on the unequal side will take one for the team in order for the organization to move forward. It may be subtle or very obvious, and take place quickly or slowly, but certain practices, systems, or procedures will be altered or will disappear completely. It is rare that two companies of equal size, influence, and market share can come together and operate successfully as a merged organization.

A plan of action, as described earlier, or a takeover is a more likely a reality. *"Corporate marriages often go wrong, but mergers of equals—in which two firms of roughly similar size combine, there is neither buyer nor target and typically no cash changes hands—account for a disproportionate share of the most notorious failures"* (Schumpter, 2014). The concept of integration as two entities coming together to create a whole is outmoded, as it doesn't withstand the short-term return mentality of today's marketplace. That doesn't mean that there isn't an opportunity to leverage the best from the companies involved, but someone will take one for the team in order to facilitate and quickly enable the pre-transformation process.

During the Petro-Canada/Suncor merger, this was probably the most difficult realization for the former Petro-Canada employees. Our ways of doing business were going to the wayside but no one bothered to tell us. If employees are not told exactly how and what will be changing for them, they will feel some level of betrayal. This betrayal can turn into a lack of trust and will impact engagement and productivity. It is my belief that the execution of the transaction could have moved forward even faster had the joint executive clearly articulated to their respective employees the real reasons for coming together and why a breakneck pace was required.

The acquisition of Petro-Canada's assets and people were very important to the success of the new Suncor. I like to think that we brought a set of crystal wine glasses for everyone at the table that allowed the guests to have something to pour their wine into. The alignment and engagement of all employees would have been even more successful if they had recognized the contributions of employees in both companies and provided clear goals, objectives, and a game plan as to how employees from both sides could work together to achieve those goals.

Context is everything. We came to the dinner party and didn't understand what meal we were going to be served and, in addition, we didn't understand the cutlery we needed to use to enjoy the meal. Our understanding of the place settings and our readiness for the meal ahead were not in sync. There is not only a need for the place setting but also for thought given as to how the meal will be served. This is called a Pre-Transformation Plan.

Building Your Pre-Transformation Plan

My own experience of the merger is that while there were consultants who attempted to understand and define the two cultures being merged, I certainly do not recall a clear and consistent acknowledgement of the emotions or concerns of the employees impacted by the merging of those two cultures. There wasn't a formal forum or a release valve for employees to express their feelings or concerns about what was happening. Other than hours in my or their leader's office venting their feelings, or consuming many drinks at the local watering holes, employees' emotions of shock or anxiety about the merger were not publicly acknowledged, yet all the expertise out there about the implementation of change in the business world tells us that unless we engage with people emotionally about the change, they can't change and nor can the change in the organizations they work in be sustained. This point is incredibly salient and important when a merger or acquisition is in play.

Once the decision is made to move forward to acquire another company, the focus goes immediately to making it happen from a legal, regulatory, and financial perspective. Those endeavors are all-encompassing for an executive team and require the full muster of the executives or owner to push it through. Those steps must happen for a merger to take place literally. However, there is another step that is required to make it happen figuratively in the hearts and minds of the employees. Not only do those in leadership need to focus on the details of creating a merged organization and new legal entity, they must focus on the equally important task of engaging the employee population on an emotional level. Being jolted into a new reality is a strange and confusing event for anyone who has been on the receiving end of a large corporate change.

Any good host wants to ensure his or her guests are comfortable during their dinner party. Coming to the table is a simple way of describing the significance of employee engagement. Executives and business owners need to be welcoming and attentive hosts if the dinner party is to be a success. They will make sure they have enough to eat and drink, are mixing well with the other guests, and will be asking if there any special needs or requests.

Think of a change plan as an executive's or business owner's way of ensuring employees are ready for the meal they are about to be served. The tricky part for any executive or business owner is to engage employees during a time when they don't know what the future holds. How can an organization leverage its most important asset—people—to start moving the integration forward when their heads are reeling from the change that's been announced and they can't yet articulate what it means for them?

Executives or business owners who are embarking on the merger or acquisition journey need to have a formalized change plan. The reason why 70% of mergers fail is due to the fact that they haven't properly set the table for transformation. Any successful dinner party is well planned, organized, and considers the needs of its guests. The same intentional approach is needed when navigating employees through the pre-transformation phase. Organizations are made up of assets, products, services, or all three. None of those in and of themselves generate revenue. A box of pencils is useful and can be used to create any number of drawings, calculations, or written words, but they obviously don't operate themselves—people do. The most effective way of unveiling how you will be serving your meal is by having an effective and meaningful change plan.

There are several change models out there and many of them provide solid advice and guidance on how to best handle corporate change. Some of the more common and accepted change models for business are Lewin's Change Management Model, Kotter's 8-Step Change Model or McKinsey's 7-S Model. All of these models address change in well-constructed, detailed steps. In my view, any good transformation plan includes three key elements: a mindset of invitation, ongoing focus, and staying connected. Let's explore these elements further in a new progressive transformation model.

Mindset of Invitation

One of the guiding principles repeated in this book is the mindset of invitation. It articulates the belief that leadership in organizations should invite employees to understand and play a part in the change. It puts the onus on executives or business owners to articulate the reasons why employees should be involved in the change. The mindset of invitation also asks executives and business owners to articulate the value employees and other stakeholders bring to the transformation ahead. Sharing the reason and purpose of those folks being at the table and the contribution they can make is a simple but effective way to demonstrate the mindset of invitation.

Ongoing Focus

Some change models reference change as a one-time event that needs to be isolated, reprogrammed, and then re-incorporated into the new company. In order to truly obtain the desired outcomes of transformation, employees and key stakeholders need to see the change as ongoing and not as a one-time event. Ongoing focus runs counter to the fast-paced, short-term return mentality of the modern marketplace. In fact, most C-suite level executives are not incentivized to maintain an ongoing focus or have their organizations in a continual state of change readiness.

"Anybody can manage short. Anybody can manage long. Balancing those two things is what management is."

– Jack Welch, Former CEO, General Electric.

Post-merger or acquisition, a continuous focus on change is

even more critical as it is the only way to accommodate for the unknowns that are sure to be uncovered as both sides of the new company come together. Change readiness also creates an environment where innovation and continuous improvement are able to take place. In real terms, an organization will need to invest that ongoing focus in three key areas. These key areas are people, processes, and technology.

People

- Make sure you have the right training available at the right time so your employees can be productive.

- Take time to make sure your employees know how things work in the new company and who in the company has the knowledge required, and is able and available to share that knowledge with those who will need it to participate in integration activities.

Process

- Do you have the right technology and/or processes to support the newly created organization? Organizations may have enabling technology or tools, but if the processes are not clearly defined, transformation will not take place.

- It will be hard to serve an elaborate meal if you don't have the right utensils or processes to get the food to the plate. You cannot automate poor business process! Similarly, if your leadership team promises an elaborate meal (value proposition) and only have a plate, knife, and fork, your guests may be confused or not trust the quality of the meal you intend to serve.

Technology

- You don't want to surprise your guests with unexpected

cutlery. Your guests may have never seen your place setting before. If that is the case, they will not understand your technology or how to use it. The guests may try to use spoons to cut steak because they have never seen knives before. Your role is to ensure they understand the technology and accompanying processes that it supports so they can engage in the transformation. Teach them how the technology works if they haven't seen it before, and train employees as soon as possible on the preferred method of operating your systems and processes.

- Take time to understand what you've acquired and whether it enables your strategy. Do a proper assessment of existing and acquired technologies. If you don't have enough of the right cutlery, you will not be able to enjoy the meal.

The points above are simple metaphors and, again, they are intended to describe the importance of having a clear view of the people, processes, and technology required to move the organization forward from the initial transaction to the transformation stage. These elements will require dedicated and continuous focus if the new company is to realize goals that support growth, cost effectiveness, and innovation.

Staying Connected

The importance of staying connected is twofold. It's about validating the results during the pre-transformation process on a regular basis. Setting meaningful goals with clear deliverables is one way executives or business owners can do this. Knowing what results or outcomes are being sought and then checking in on those daily, weekly, or quarterly creates accountability and a sense of belonging in the new company.

When employees are held accountable to specific results and

outcomes, they will work together regardless of differences to achieve them. Trust in leadership and its vision for the future can also take a leap forward if there is a realistic and timely approach to tracking and measuring the success of achieving those goals. The second part of staying connected is about the need for us as human beings to belong and to have a sense of community. Showing appreciation and thanking your employees by bringing them together to celebrate the achievement of the results is an ideal way to build a sense of belonging and community. A key component of building community is acknowledgement. Staying connected is also about regularly recognizing and validating employees' efforts. Staying connected to your guests throughout the duration of your dinner party ensures that they will want to come back to your table again and again.

Notwithstanding which side of the equation your organization is on, be aware that as an executive or business owner, you will need to navigate the shifting landscape and the changes that result for your employees if you want them to be a part of a newly merged organization. Being authentic and honest about how one group taking one for the team will enable the corporate vision is a way to ensure your employees are able to come to the table ready to participate in the new company. Having a plan for transformation is how any executive or business owner can begin and sustain the employee-engagement process. Setting the table is an important precursor before serving the transformation meal ahead.

"If people believe in what you believe and if they believe in what you stand for, they are more likely to become engaged. And, in my mind, the number one job of the CEO or senior leadership is to facilitate that engagement."

– Margot Micallef, QC, President, Oliver Capital Partners

Key Insights

- Someone will take one for the team. One company's way will dominate and it is important to articulate that clearly to your employee base. Be authentic and honest about how one group "taking one for the team" will enable the corporate vision.

- Employees need to know how things are going to work as a soon as possible.

- Stay connected. Make sure there are meaningful ways to measure results and that your employees are doing ok.

CHAPTER 6

Serving Your Menu

Working Together – Making the Meal Come to Life

The table is now set and your guests have arrived and are getting excited about the meal they are about to be served. At the best dinner parties, a lot of thought and preparation go into preparing the meal. How each dish will be prepared and served and in what order is carefully orchestrated to ensure the appetizer, main course, dessert, and everything in between is served properly and on time.

At a grand dinner party each dish creates anticipation for the next and delights the guests around the table. The work required to prepare for such a party is significant and can take a long time. The theme, the invitation, the welcome, and the place settings all require a plan to achieve the outcome of the party. Your dinner has to be planned, communicated, and executed flawlessly.

Think of integration as the preparation of the meal that will be served at the dinner party. Integration focuses on many activities to create a shared outcome. It demands the same focus and dedication to ensure it paves the way for transformation. It requires heavy lifting and a resolute focus on the results and behaviours that model the new company's values. Pre-transformation and the integration activities that support it are disruptive and, in many cases, not pragmatically contemplated or planned for. Like the chaos of creating a grand meal in the kitchen, the upheaval it creates has to be anticipated, monitored, and managed.

Even if the executive leadership team or business owner is doing those things regularly, they may still find that some guests don't want to stay at the table for the whole meal. Learning how to work together and share the meal is the bridge that gets the new company from vision to reality. The coming together of employees is just as important as the meal itself. Depending on your specific merger or acquisition, many will stay for the entire meal, but it may be difficult for them along the way. The reality is that employees tasked with executing the integration process are subjected for a time to a strange kind of existence. They don't know what's ahead, they are going to be handed many challenging deliverables to be completed within tight timelines, and their loyalty to the new company is in a fragile state. Employees who are involved in integration activities will experience it as a challenging and difficult time that includes hard work, and as a time where they will be seriously contemplating their skills and abilities and whether they will fit into the new organization.

Any good chef or home cook knows that the ingredients and how they are put together to create new dishes is a matter of *balance*—one that consists of solid recipes, careful preparation of ingredients, regular minding of those dishes as they come together, and ensuring those meals are served just in time. Bringing different guests together can be a risk and how you treat them and orient them to the meal you are about to serve will mean the difference between a successful dinner party, or one with delays or an unsatisfying meal. Some people will leave when they see the table setting or whom they are sitting next to. You may not have enough place settings for all the guests initially. Some will not be able to experience the meal as you intended. They will be deciding if they can digest the meal that is being served. The experience of working through the ups and downs of pre-transformation to create a new path forward is a turning point for employees, but one where they and the new company and its vision can succeed. Before you can have your employees working together, you need to be mindful of what integration will be like for them.

There are four key things needed for a successful integration. If you don't pay attention to them, your meal is hooped! Managing the quest for synergy, monitoring the use of consultants, balancing the heavy lifting integration requires, and determining who should stay are key pieces of the integration puzzle that executives and business owners will have to put in place if they want to make the deal come to life. Ultimately, each employee will have to make a decision about what their contribution will be and an employee's decision to stay or leave the company will emerge as the new company begins to take shape. If you are leading employees through integration activities, you will need to help them understand the work ahead, create a sense of urgency to accomplish clear and measurable deliverables, and provide opportunities to develop a community within the new company.

Don't Rush the Meal – Managing the Quest for

Synergy

Synergy Quest. Sounds like an amazing online game that your kids want to play, doesn't it? If I could create a game for CEOs that would help them play out the quest for synergy, I could dominate the corporate and gaming world! In the game, CEOs would have to find ways to leverage assets, integration, shareholders, revenue growth, strategy, *and* inspire their people in order to win the game and achieve *synergy*. Sound exciting and extremely difficult? You bet it is.

Merged companies can die under the weight of trying to create a combined effort that is greater than the sum of its previous parts. When a merger or acquisition takes place, the race for ever-elusive synergies can cause executive leadership or a business owner to push hard to show the marketplace their newly found efficiency. The drive towards metrics that show quick returns to shareholders or investors often creates a false sense of accomplishment, and when examined over a period of time, those accomplishments cannot withstand scrutiny and the pace of change. The execution of a merger or acquisition is multi-layered and the complexity of the undertaking needs to be examined carefully. Directing the efforts of duplicate workforces, dual or multiple processes and streamlining technologies and practices can be incredibly difficult but necessary.

Synergy as a key driver behind a merger or acquisition is so difficult to achieve because you have two organizations trying to enter into a marriage of sorts without really dating each other. Consider dating in the North American context for a moment. Would you accept or offer a proposal of marriage to someone after you had read his or her online profile only? You haven't met the person. You've only just seen a picture and read about 250 words or less that they have told you about themselves. Of course, we all know how honest online profiles are. You would likely agree that the odds of a marriage that starts out that way being successful would be slim. However, in a business context, companies essentially do the same thing. They have their legal and finance teams doing a limited amount of screening (online dating service). They have access to market data and information on assets (online profile) and, based on

limited and often regulated access to information, the decision is made to proceed with a merger or acquisition.

As per most mergers or acquisitions, the quest to create synergies, maximize capital and increase shareholder value are at the top of a long list of buzzwords used to engage employees. That was certainly the case within the first year of the merger I experienced. For example, basic processes that we took for granted became foreign to many of us in the newly merged world. I think back to a basic HR process: recruitment. Some of us didn't know the system or process to use to hire people or if our clients had authorization to hire new people. If they did have authorization, what were the steps needed to create a position, advertise the job, and make an offer?

Many of us had to learn on the fly and expend a lot of additional effort to help our clients do the things that they needed to do to move their business ahead. The executives that engineered the merger were quite confident that the two companies were very similar and would achieve synergy quickly, but on the ground it proved to be more challenging to execute. Merging organizations need to map out key business processes in order to first identify what the key enablers of a company's critical workflows are and truly understand what is needed to ensure there will be business continuity until processes are merged or improved over time. It's like creating an emergency response plan around processes. More and more companies are building an emergency response or business continuity plan should there be a business interruption, pandemic, or disaster. They do so to protect their assets, ensure key work can take place, and manage liabilities. I would categorize a merger or an acquisition as a significant business interruption and recommend that organizations focus on the few key critical processes that they need to maintain while there is significant upheaval going on due to the merger or acquisition. This is particularly important when you consider the functional groups that support a business.

Human Resources, Legal, Finance, and Supply Chain all need to be a part of a business continuity plan during a merger or acquisition or else the process of integration will start off on the wrong footing. In my merger experience, our "marriage" was unfolding and we were now discovering the details about how our new "partner" worked.

Synergy is an outcome, not a goal, so don't cut your nose off to spite your face for stakeholders. It's important to manage the menu and not rush the dinner and skip the appetizers to get to the main course or dessert too quickly. In other words, don't join in the race for so-called synergies that aren't real or—even worse—aren't sustainable. There is nothing more deceptive than showing cost savings and using creative efficiency metrics six months after a merger or acquisition for the market and then 24 months later going through the exercise of cost cutting, staff reductions, rehires, or scaling back your business plan because those cost-saving synergies were not real to begin with.

Take the time to develop sustainable ways to measure success that demonstrate progress against your goals. Make sure your appetizers and main course (value proposition) or way of doing business (processes and technology) are prepared to serve when they are ready, not when they are half-formed or half-baked— pun intended! A newly merged or acquired organization must determine what true efficiency means to them rather than seeking synergy. Many organizations want to show the market a boost to the stock price for shareholders or investors to show savings and that is not an unreasonable aim.

True share value or cost savings come from taking a thoughtful and measured approach to defining and creating what reliability, efficiency, and sustainability will look like in the new organization. Full realization of synergies requires front-line employees and leaders to engage in full disclosure of processes and practices to assess where synergies may or may not lie. The cost of true integration is tremendous in terms of time, understanding the work, and appreciating what exactly individuals do within the operations or corporately. But the cost of not effectively integrating systems, processes, practices, and procedures is far greater. If you look at companies years after their respective mergers or acquisitions, many of them are still working on effectively integrating their systems, processes, and ways of doing business, even though the increased shareholder value derived from synergies was promised at the outset.

If we think back to our recently married online-dating couple, the rules of engagement need to be determined. Do they focus on "growth" by having some kids and, if so, will they create their own or "acquire" them by adoption? They may already have multiple children between them already and will focus their energy internally on growing them to be successful human beings or "ventures." Yet another option may be for them to not "grow" at all, but to focus on "reducing or managing costs" by not having any kids and banking extra cash for things like better Christmas gifts (dividends) for the relatives. These decisions are not unlike the decisions CEOs or business owners need to make to chart the course of their organizations.

A great meal takes time to prepare and time to serve. Know your value proposition. What does your company do better than any other company? What technologies, systems, or practices give you a competitive advantage? Make sure you have the right tools and processes, and give your guests enough time to know what they are. The best meals are comprised of many parts served at a reasonable pace and in sequence. Know what you are serving and make sure your employees do too, so they can enjoy and help serve the meal in the future.

Hire the Right Caterer – Manage Consultants Wisely

A toothpaste factory had a problem: they sometimes shipped empty boxes without the tube inside. This was due to the way the production line was set up, and people with experience in designing production lines will tell you how difficult it is to have everything happen with timings so precise that every single unit coming out of it is perfect 100% of the time. Small variations in the environment (which can't be controlled in a cost-effective fashion) mean you must have quality assurance checks smartly distributed across the line so that customers all the way down to the supermarket don't get cranky and buy another product instead.

Understanding how important that was, the CEO of the toothpaste factory got the top people in the company together and they decided to start a new project, in which they would hire an external engineering company to solve their empty boxes problem, as their engineering department was already too stretched to take on any extra effort. The project followed the usual process: budget and project-sponsor allocated, RFP, third-parties selected, and six months (and $8 million) later they had a fantastic solution, on time, on budget, high quality, and everyone in the project patted themselves on the back. They solved the problem by using high-tech precision scales that would sound a bell and flash lights whenever a toothpaste box would weigh less than it should. The line would stop, and someone had to walk over and yank the defective box out of it, pressing another button when done to restart the line. A while later, the CEO decides to have a look at the ROI of the project: amazing results! No empty boxes ever shipped out of the factory after the *scales were put in place. Very few customer complaints and they were gaining market share. That's some money well spent, he says, before looking closely at the other statistics in the report.*

It turns out the number of defects picked up by the scales was 0 after three weeks of production use. It should've been picking up at least a dozen a day, so maybe there was something wrong with the report. He filed a bug against it, and after some investigation, the engineers come back saying the report was actually correct. The scales really weren't picking up any defects, because all boxes that got to that point in the conveyor belt were good. Puzzled, the CEO travels down to the factory, and walks up to the part of the line where the precision scales were installed. A few feet before the scale, there was a $20 desk fan, blowing the empty boxes out of the belt and into a bin.

"Oh, that," says one of the workers, "one of the guys put it there 'cause he was tired of walking over every time the bell rang."

– Alan Barfoot, Georgia Tech Enterprise Innovation Center

The toothpaste story above is a funny but very telling one that speaks to the double-edged sword value that consultants bring. They are like the hired wait staff at your dinner party. They can be a great help in taking care of your guests and serving your meal, or they can be intrusive, interrupt your guests, and disrupt the flow of your party. Each merger or acquisition is different and requires some flexibility with a view to scalability early on to make it stick. The amount of integration work required depends on whether you are acquiring assets, people, or both.

If your company is only looking to buy assets, the integration activities will likely focus on bringing the existing operation into the current fold. If those processes are working well and are scalable, the negative impact of getting bigger will be limited because they will not be encumbered by people matters. When assets and people are being brought into the mix, the amount of heavy lifting will increase significantly. My observations over a number of years in various organizations is that employees within a company usually always have a very clear understanding of what works and what doesn't. More importantly, they are the best equipped to solve their own problems.

Large consulting firms bring experience and tools for merger and acquisition activities and have step-by-step processes to help organizations integrate after the transaction. However, they don't have complete knowledge about the companies they serve and their templates, tools, and processes are standard and not always fit for purpose. The reason the toothpaste story is so compelling is because, in many cases, organizations already have the tools that they need to create their own solutions and solve their own problems, but they choose not to because they don't recognize their own in-house expertise. Organizations who decide to use consultants or consulting firms should use them cautiously and be aware of the possible benefits and pitfalls they can present.

Many large consulting firms were deployed to make the Petro-Canada/Suncor merger work and the integration would not have been completed without their help due to the sheer size of the companies involved. Regardless of the size of the merger or acquisition, if consultants or consultancy firms are to be used it is critical that executives and business owners manage the following:

1. *Ensure There is a Focus on Productivity.* Make sure your employees are working for themselves and not for the consultants! During the first critical weeks immediately after the Petro-Canada/Suncor merger, there were several requests by consultants for employee information to be

entered into complex spreadsheets and presentations that we didn't understand, nor would we ever use. They often wanted this information within hours of the request to ensure they met their project timelines and deliverables. I know that those consultants were committed to producing the results they were hired for, but they seemed oblivious to the fact that their partners in HR at both companies still had their day jobs in addition to the integration activities they needed us to help them with.

We were tasked with helping leaders make serious decisions that were going to impact employees' jobs, their teams, and ultimately their careers. Many of us had never experienced the relentlessness of the workload or the harshness of having to let so many employees go so rapidly over the course of days and weeks. The impact of this was emotionally taxing on each of us. The frustration of being asked for information we didn't have combined with the exhaustion of helping leaders let whole teams of people go on a daily basis was overwhelming. Make sure your teams are focused on the right work. Don't let your consultants take over your party.

2. *Manage Unintended Bias.* The new company's leadership must own the vision and communicate what they want it to look like as clearly and quickly as possible to both employees and consultants, or they may end up footing a very large bill for processes it does not need or will not use. Bias can be directed against acquired employees or the executives or owners themselves. Consultants are brought in because they can be objective and are keenly adept at altering methods and approaches to ensure they are meeting the client's needs, which usually means a change in approach and, of course, more billable time! To be clear, I don't wish to demonize consultants for the hard and often valuable work they do, but partnering with the right kind of consultants who take

the time to understand the multiple layers of a business and the key players they are supporting is critical in moving the organization forward post-merger or acquisition.

It is important to go slow in order to go fast to implement those few key things that will enable employees to engage quickly during the initial stages of integration. Complicated organizational structures or process models may be exciting or promise better results, but right after a merger or acquisition, simplicity adds the most value. Good consultants provide the right amount of transactional expertise that *facilitates* the transformation needed. If consultants are to be used, they must partner with existing employees and be clear about what a successful outcome looks like for the new organization. If the output of a consultancy firm's transition plan is not scalable or properly executed and owned by the employees who remain, true transformation cannot begin to take place.

3. *Ask Employees for Their Input.* When organizations use their own employees to solve their own problems, take accountability for those solutions, and share their knowledge, a merged or acquired organization has a significantly increased chance of success. The toothpaste story makes this point beautifully. Used correctly, consultants in partnership can help enable and accelerate this process, but ultimately they can't own it, nor should they. This is the difference between completing a series of transactions that drive deliverables, and building the accountability and trust of employees that create transformative change within the organization. Consultants are there to help organize and execute the transaction. The horsepower they provide should be focused on the many detailed and necessary activities required to make the deal work.

Make sure the consultants you hire can help you serve your

menu correctly. Partner wisely with consultants so they don't take over your dinner party. Ensure your employees are empowered to own the solutions and outcomes of integration.

Digesting the Meal – Managing the Hard Work of Integration

The act of integration is messy, complicated, difficult, and requires unwavering focus. The turmoil and uncertainty a merger or acquisition creates brings to light the fears and aspirations of employees and those that lead them.

Suncor and Petro-Canada were two completely different organizations that came together so quickly that I had to buckle my seatbelt and hold on tight for the bumpy ride ahead. The speed of the transaction felt like two cars crashing into one another, and the disorder and disruption that resulted happened at an accelerated pace. Within six weeks, we were charging down the path to integrate and there was no time to be wasted. What remains after a merger or acquisition can be planned for, but not necessarily predicted. A merger or acquisition is intended to be the beginning of something bigger and better that will ultimately result in the ending of something that once was. The truth is, there is no time to prepare for the intense level of hard work that will be expected of employees in the weeks and months that follow the merger or acquisition, especially the mental, emotional, and physical toll it can take on employees to make the merger or acquisition a success.

Distinct Change of Energy

For many employees, going from doing things well to not being as effective is an added difficulty that they may not have been expecting. Most employees take pride in being able to do a job well and share their expertise. This is not always the case right after a merger or acquisition. Part of the reality of merged life in a new organization is that you may not be able to create and leverage the same energy and enthusiasm you once had. You may now be working with different people that you don't know, or in a different role than the one you used to have. This can be a good thing, but it can also cause you to shift gears for a while until you can navigate the new landscape.

It takes time to adjust to your new location, co-workers, and way of doing things, not to mention the time it takes to digest and understand the new corporate-speak that inevitably follows from the newly formed executive team. The ability to exert discretionary effort is much more difficult at times at the beginning of a merger or acquisition, particularly if you and your company are the ones who have been acquired. According to BusinessDictionary.com, discretionary effort is the *"difference in the level of effort one is capable of bringing to an activity or a task, and the effort required only to get by or make do."* In Human Resources, the discretionary effort of employees is often used as a measure of engagement and productivity.

For example, if an employee has had a busy week of meetings and was unable to complete tasks or assignments during the week, and chooses to come into the office on the weekend to catch up and prepare for the next week, that could be seen as an example of discretionary effort. Some people think that is part of doing their job, but many managers in an organization would not say to an employee that they must use days off to accomplish work goals. Some employees may choose not to expend additional effort and still meet their goals and complete work assignments. Whether you agree that discretionary effort is a measure of engagement or not, it can only be exerted when an employee is emotionally connected to the work they are performing.

Ownership of one's work is not just a reflection of pride in doing a good job, but is equally about exceeding expectations while relishing in a positive feeling of accomplishment. I still find it incredible that however adaptable we are as human beings, we know when we connect to something in our life that shifts our consciousness—whether it is in a relationship, or in a work experience like a merger or acquisition, it makes a memorable impression that stays with us forever, good or bad.

Once a merger or acquisition, or significant business change in the organization has been announced, and the hands have all been shaken and the photos taken, employees may find themselves in an awkward space of being forced to let go of what they were doing that was familiar and comfortable and that they had control over. They will have to quickly step-up and take responsibility for brand new experiences that hold them in nervous anticipation without having a clue as to what they are supposed to do next. Feelings of confusion, grief, anxiousness, or even excitement may be experienced.

Remember when they enter into that void they are only human and can only achieve results depending on what they are capable of enduring. I'm sure that when executives, business owners, and boards convene in planning mergers or acquisitions, they discuss the impact people will experience when merging two companies, especially when their cultures are very different from one another. What I am not convinced of is their ability to fully understand how challenging, disruptive, and potentially devastating this time of change can be for employees. Deciphering and rendering the change in the right way so they can drive key actions to help their new organization succeed is key.

John Kotter's 8-Step Change Model (1996) is useful here as it: "[…] *emphasises engaging with people emotionally because unless people themselves change, changes made in the organisational environment do not persist.*" Kotter's model is particularly astute as it tells us that we can't even begin to acclimate to, or accept change unless there is an acknowledgement and understanding of the power of people's emotions, and that without this acknowledgement and understanding you cannot create a climate of change. Astute executives know this is important and will want to ensure that the direction of the new organization is set quickly and deftly. Recognizing and addressing the change is an important step an executive or business owner can take to help manage the change of energy.

Wear and Tear

There is a certain level of wear and tear that occurs when you are experiencing a large-scale business change. The wear and tear can be physical, mental, or emotional. Deloitte, one of the large consulting firms retained to handle corporate integration processes, indicates in their White Paper on post-merger integration (PMI), *Post-merger integration when perfection is the enemy of good* that, "Nothing is slow and steady in PMI. You must prepare your staff for the reality that is integration. It will be intense, demanding, and exhausting. It is up to PMI leaders to figure out how to make the process rewarding. You must motivate by knowing when to press the gas and when to let up." Truer words were never spoken by consultants!

What I remember most vividly is the physical toll that the merger took on me. Over the first 12 months post-announcement, I experienced lack of sleep, chronic aches and pains in my shoulders, hair loss, and other ailments related to stress. The long, chaotic days followed by less-than-restful nights cumulatively resulted in a mind and body that was a bit worse for wear. I distinctly remember many conversations with family and friends about the workload and hearing how tired and weary I sounded. I am grateful for their patience and support. At that time, I could have easily carried my own orchestra of violins with me for all the whining I was doing to my family and friends, but in retrospect, I believe I needed to release some of the angst and, quite frankly, the *stress* that I was experiencing. The amount of change and resulting stress, no matter what kind, has a direct connection to how you feel physically, mentally, and emotionally.

Your employees may notice changes in their appetite and energy level. They may also respond to situations with less patience, take longer to make simple decisions, and have difficulty focusing on complex or even regular tasks. Many of these responses are normal and are definitely part of coping with change. As an executive or business owner, providing informal and formal support is essential in combating this. Ensuring employees have the opportunity to talk with their supervisors or with Human Resources in a safe environment will help them gain and maintain perspective as the work progresses. Providing access to employee and family assistance counseling services is also a more formal way to ensure employees have the opportunity to get the support they and their families may need during the long days of integration.

Many of my colleagues and clients experienced wear and tear in their own ways. In a recent conversation with a colleague about that time, she recalled that we all looked pretty terrible during integration. We were worn out and had many demands on us that some of us were having a hard time coping with. The demands of making the merger work in human resources were huge, chaotic at times, and very taxing on those who had to understand and implement the changes. We were trying to balance our desire to be effective to our clients, understand the changes that were coming almost daily, and maintain our energy level after staffing most of the new Suncor in just six weeks. Many of us had varying levels of difficulty coping with it all.

During those first few difficult months, a number of my co-workers left the organization, as they could not handle the stress and strain of what they were going through. They had reached a limit and were no longer prepared to sustain the wear and tear on their minds and bodies in order to cope, and decided to leave the organization. I still miss many of them and wonder how they would have faired if they stayed and continued to endure the grind of integration a bit longer. They decided quite early on whether they should stay or go. My own way of coping was to simplify my life. Initially, this was not a conscious decision, but one that I gravitated to naturally to maintain a sense of control in my life. I thought about my own hierarchy of needs and determined what was most important to me. My health and mental wellbeing were the first priority.

I started exercising more regularly and kept my activities fairly routine and simple for a period of time.

This decision enabled me to maintain and, eventually, restore balance. To keep your employees' reservoirs filled up, they may require something different. Exercise, nutrition, faith practices, hobbies, family, and friends are just some of the ways that may be helpful to them. Provide opportunities for dialogue about what's working in the integration and what's not. Creating a sense of community is needed to help employees feel like they belong. That community is the new company. Being conscious of the wear and tear on employees and providing informal and formal care and concern will go a long way. In addition, delivering messages that confirm "we are all in this together" regularly, is helpful and reconfirms the idea that the hard work is important and appreciated.

Should They Stay or Should They Go – A Checklist for Leaders

Employees' relationship with their employer is multi-faceted and complex. It will have high and low points, and most certainly test their assumptions about who they are and what they have to offer. After a significant event such as a merger or acquisition, employees may find themselves in a place where they are not sure whether or not they want to stay in a working relationship with their current employer.

Like any other relationship that we enter into, there may be an event or series of events that cause them to pause, reflect, and re-consider their desire to stay, especially during the upheaval of integrating companies. Your employees may find themselves wondering if they should stay and be a part of the pre-transformation activities in the short term or even with the new company going forward. You want to ensure your guests are going to stay to enjoy the meal you are about to serve. More importantly, you have to take the opportunity to influence their decision and confirm the value proposition that the merger or acquisition presents to them and their careers.

Below is a checklist that line-leaders and supervisors, specifically, can use to help their employees confirm and/or reaffirm their fit in the new organization. Use this checklist to help employees gain clarity during a time when they most need it.

☐ *Do they truly understand the vision of the new company?* Does the corporate vision make sense to them now and can they get on board with the executive team or business owner's long-term vision and value proposition? Can they see where their work will help further that vision? In most cases, this will take time to discern as it may change and shift. Employees should have an initial line of sight to where the company is going and where they want to be within the new company.

☐ *Do their values match the new culture?* Values are not just those ideas or concepts that a company *says* is important to them, they are what a company actually *does and rewards* on a consistent basis. Company values are often not worth the ink they are written with! They tend to be aspirational platitudes that are attached to empty or vague vision and mission statements.

Consider when you first met your significant other for a moment. At some point in the relationship, you discovered that you had shared values that enabled you to progress the relationship. The mutual set of values and/or beliefs eventually provided a common footing on which the relationship could stand. This is not much different than the relationship employees may have with the newly merged or acquired company.

Employee loyalty is fragile during integration and they are looking for tangible evidence that the new company is going to make good on their newly created values. Pay very close attention to your line-managers and supervisors, and their behaviour during integration. They are the folks that will be providing evidence to employees on a daily basis that the company's values are real and meaningful. Simply put, an employee should be able to see an alignment between the values that they hold near and dear, and those of the new company.

☐ *Is there a fit between the employee and the emerging culture?* How would you describe your emerging culture? Is the culture authoritative or consultative? If an employee likes to work autonomously and make quick decisions, while the new company is very hierarchical in nature with many levels of approval required to make decisions, he or she will have to adjust or it is likely that over time frustration will result. Recognize and know what work environment allows and encourages your employees to make their best contribution.

☐ *Can the employee make a significant contribution?* Is there a realistic opportunity for employees to grow skills/career or share their specific knowledge and expertise? In many cases, there are loads of opportunities to develop an employee's capabilities further or try something new that they might not have had the chance to try before.

In my own journey through a merger, I know that I learned a great deal and know much more now than I did before the merger. Even if their confidence is shaken a bit, encourage your employees to start taking inventory of their skills, capabilities and contributions. If that seems daunting for them, have them think about the things they like to do.

Getting clear about the value of their skills, capabilities, and contributions will help them determine if they fit in the new company.

Look for the growth/learning opportunity for them and their teams. Every employee has something to offer and so does every company. Help employees be clear about what they have to offer and what you want them to contribute to the new organization.

☐ *What level is their Personal Reservoir at?* Do your employees have enough resilience, tolerance, and appetite left for more change and disruption? Can they handle long periods of ambiguity? There is no shame in admitting that they are just plain tired. Perhaps they have been through several small mergers or acquisitions and have change fatigue. Maybe their personal lives are at a crossroads and they need stability in their work life. Taking a moment to help employees consider and assess the level of their own personal reservoirs is something that you can contribute to, and it will help your employees make good decisions about staying or going. If you find them currently disengaged due to change fatigue, the new company's values don't resonate with them, and they are not energized or enthusiastic about the new company, does stepping onto this new path really make sense for them?

As an executive or business owner, you need to give some thought to whether or not the teams you lead have enough muster left to make a contribution in the new organization. If you don't think they have enough gas left in the tank, you will need to help them find ways to top up and restore their reservoir and/or help them make plans to exit in a respectful manner with dignity.

☐ *Are they open to possibilities?* Are your employees comfortable with considering other types of roles within the new company? Is the opportunity at hand interesting, exciting, and challenging? Can you offer them opportunities to learn something new or leverage their current knowledge and expertise in a different setting? If they are solid contributors who aren't looking to become leaders, are they comfortable doing the same type of work they are doing now for the next few years? There is no right or wrong answer, simply a personal choice to be made.

If you see the landscape ahead changing to the point there will not be a need for an employee's skills and capabilities, help them start looking at other options for their careers. There are truly no shortages of opportunities post-merger for an employee regardless of job level or title even if they end up not being in the newly created company. The decision to stay open to the possibilities is ultimately one that only the employee can make, but it is a mindset that you as an executive or business owner will want to cultivate by reinforcing their value and the need for their skills.

Making Your Dinner Party a Success

Transformation is the ultimate goal of any merger or acquisition. Simply stated, the act of transformation is moving from the present state to a desired future state. The only way that real, true transformation can occur is if there is a conscious and deliberate design to achieve it. Mergers or acquisitions fail because the majority of the energy is focused on the transaction and there is not a deliberate focus on building and executing a plan for the transformation. Executives and business owners own the responsibility for and trajectory of the transformation. So what does that mean?

Leaders need to be resolutely focused on the management of

their employees as they navigate through the pre-transformation stage of a merger or acquisition. The executives' or business owner's role is to be transparent about the reason for coming together, share as clear a vision as possible, and provide employees with as much support as needed to carry the heavy weight of integration as they embark on putting the new company together. They need to be deliberate in making large-scale corporate changes like mergers better for employees.

Leveraging the skills and capabilities of people effectively during a time of change is equally as important as increasing shareholder/investor value, gaining market share, or managing costs and cash flow. If you're going to do the deal, make sure that the betterment of all of the company assets is considered, including your people. Transforming shareholder/investor value, market share, and productivity to a positive effect are some of the universally sought-after outcomes of mergers or acquisitions, so there should be a focus on transforming people too. Employees are the key enablers of transformation and, ultimately, enablers of its success. Here are simple things you can do to make your dinner party a success:

1. *Articulate and Confirm the Value proposition.* When hosting a dinner party, a good host will always ask the guests how they are doing, if they have enough to eat, or if they would like to have some more to eat. In a merger or acquisition, the same holds true. Know your value proposition and how your employees can and should contribute to it. They should know why they are there and what they can do to help the integration process. Executives and business owners need to check in and ask for feedback, whether formally via a focus group or survey, or informally by having team meetings and walking the halls or work site. This is an important step in ensuring an effective integration process is taking place.

2. *Manage the Quest for Synergy.* Executives or business owners who declare the way in which they wish to conduct business early—and have a realistic method of measurement—have a better chance of creating the efficiency they seek during integration. Manage the chaos in the kitchen so your guests can enjoy the meal. The new company will have a better chance of eventually creating the efficiency they seek. A company that is embroiled in deciding whose way is the best will waste valuable time and resources early on when their time is best served executing on post-merger or acquisition initiatives and integration activities. Choosing one way over the other needs to be balanced with the intent of deciding what the best options are for the *new* organization.

To accelerate the integration process, it is prudent to recognize and take stock of the full value and appropriate usage of the assets and employee talent being acquired. Serve the dinner with a measured sense of urgency. People don't want to linger over appetizers too long. Make the tough decisions of integration quickly and with a sense of purpose. If you have set your table correctly, it will not be hard to find quick wins and give employees the tools and the autonomy to achieve them. Build a sense of community and belonging through achievement. Link results back to the vision. A meal is served in increments, not all at once, so manage the pace and path to achieving synergy.

3. *Take Care of Your Employees.* Remember the elements of a quality Pre-Transformation Plan. Always employ a Mindset of Invitation, Ongoing Focus, and Stay Connected. Ask how your employees are doing regularly. Make sure you support, engage, and encourage employees while they are doing the heavy lifting needed to integrate. Employees should not only digest the meal, they should have the opportunity to enjoy each course even if they never experience them again. The

work of integration will leave your employees exhausted, but the meal or end result you serve should be satisfying and served by attentive and accommodating hosts. Each guest should finish their meal satiated and be excited about the delicious dessert they are about to be a part of.

"One of the biggest challenges you have when you integrate an asset and people is they don't understand the processes; they don't understand the organization. You need to have somebody that can be the filter or liaison between the organization and the new entities and people being integrated."

– Perry Schuldhaus, President, Enbridge Income Fund Holdings Inc. (ENF)

Key Insights

- Manage the quest for synergy. Synergy is an outcome, not a goal.

- Don't invite your employees to the dinner party and not serve them the meal you promised, or let them rummage through your cabinets to make their own dinner.

- Don't leave integration activities to chance or up to employees. Serve them the meal and provide support to help them digest it.

- Having your guests come together effectively to do the work is just as important as the meal you serve. Create a sense of community. They will need it to get through the heavy lifting integration requires.

TRANSFORMATION

CHAPTER 7

Dessert

Planning for Your New Culture

Our grand dinner party ends with a delicious and memorable dessert. Dessert can be a decadent and special part of the meal. It's one of the most important parts of a fantastic dinner party, because it is the last course served and leaves a lasting memory of a wonderful gathering. Dessert is a complement to the delicious courses you have served throughout the dinner party. A good host will ensure that the dessert complements the dinner party theme. You wouldn't serve a decadent croque-en-bouche (tower of creampuffs bound with delicate threads of caramel) at a southern-style barbeque party.

To ensure your dessert complements the rest of your meal, it needs to be planned and prepared first. In this context, dessert represents the newly created organization's culture. It should be delicious, inviting, rich, and something your employees want to experience over and over again. In order to achieve that result, culture, like dessert, has to be thought of well in advance of the rest of your dinner party. At the best dinner parties, dessert is prepared before the guests arrive, not during the party. If we liken dessert to an organization's culture, why then is it so often left to be created or evolve on its own?

We know that a lack of cultural integration can make or break mergers or acquisitions, so why do executives, business owners, and corporate boards leave it out of the transaction equation? One doesn't have to look too far to see where this oversight has significantly impacted the success of a merger or acquisition. The failed merger of Daimler-Chrysler shared earlier is an example of a merger where there wasn't a plan for the two companies to come together and consciously build a new culture for the new organization, and so Daimler-Chrysler failed to transform. Therein lies the opportunity to do things differently and to do things better. Don't get left behind in 20th century thinking around mergers and acquisitions. Plan for the success of your merger or acquisition and the transformation you seek.

As a business owner or executive, you must start planning the culture you wish to create the minute you start to plan your merger or acquisition strategy. As a business leader, the choice is yours to make. You can transform your business poorly by leaving the matter of employee engagement and culture to unfold on its own, or you can shape the transformation right from the start. Be a modern business leader and declare the culture you wish to create and start planning it immediately! The impact of doing so is that you will have productive, engaged employees who will help you maximize your investment faster.

Transformation takes time. The good news is that each of the steps that have been outlined in this book for your dinner party will increase your chances of success. Those steps will help you create a foundation to build a productive and sustainable culture post-merger or acquisition.

Plan the Culture You Want to Create

Think of the culture you want to create as a tall, beautifully iced layer cake. Each layer is delicious and builds upon the next. Every part of your grand dinner party helps build the foundation of a culture. How your employees experience the invitation, the welcome, and the meal itself build upon each other to show positive and tangible proof that the culture you are trying to create is real. There are many descriptions and explanations of culture out there and most of them describe it as a set of beliefs, customs, behaviours, or ways of thinking for certain societies or groups.

All of these definitions are accurate, but I believe that there is a critical and fundamental piece missing. Culture is deeper than beliefs, customs, and behaviours. Those descriptions represent the physical manifestations of what culture *is*. What is missing is what culture *does*. Culture, in this model, is where values, community, belonging, opportunity, and growth layer upon each other to create an unforgettable imprint on those who work within an organization. That imprint is powerful and stays with an employee for years, possibly forever.

If culture has the kind of power that will make or break an organization's success and keep employees engaged or drive them away, it is worth paying attention to! On a micro level, if you've had the opportunity to work in an organization where you felt your values were matched and honoured, made important connections and friends, had some career opportunities and successes, made a contribution, and grew your skills or those of others, then you have experienced culture as a dessert worth having over and over again. A great work culture cultivates your mind, actualizes your personal and professional goals, *and* pays your bills. At the macro level, in an organization where the values are clearly defined and upheld, effort is put forth to create a community of employees who believe in the organization's strategy. Those employees, in turn, seize the opportunity to contribute to creating a successful outcome for the company. The result is growth for the organization and is achieved when the company experiences increased competitive position, better market share, and higher revenue and profitability.

Values

The first fabulous layer of the culture dessert is values. It is the foundation layer of the cake that all of the other layers are built upon. Business owners and executives need to be clear and committed to the values they want to embed in the newly created organization. Those values need to be determined right at the beginning of the transaction phase as they will be the base upon which the rest of your culture will be built. In the transaction phase when the details are being worked out, being clear about the values that define the new company is critical.

Why is this so important? Values let your employees and customers understand what your company is about and what it stands for. You want to consciously define the values that will drive the performance of the newly created organization. In addition, you want to define what behaviours will be rewarded to ingrain the values and culture of the new organization. How you live and breathe your company's values is what will give your employees a clear sense of what the company stands for. Values are an invitation to your employees. They are the part of the invitation that creates connection to common goals, aligns beliefs, and helps define ways of working within a business.

When a business owner or executive declares the company's values and are visible stewards of those values, they create an environment of trust. As an HR professional, my belief is that the best work environments for employees are ones where their own personal values are aligned with those of their employer. When that alignment does not exist, employees will not believe that their skills, abilities, or contributions matter.

Your invitation should attract the kind of employees your company needs, entice them to stay, and invite others to come along too. Determine which values will drive the performance and success of the organization so you have a solid foundation for your dessert.

Community

The second delicious layer of your dessert is community. You've sent out an enticing invitation and crafted the values of the new company. Values alone cannot create a healthy culture post-merger or acquisition. When you merge or acquire a new company, business owners and executives need to welcome both new and existing employees to the new company. They need to on-board them to the way the new company will operate, and honour the contributions of employees from both sides. In my merger experience, I didn't immediately feel the sense of being welcomed or being part of the new company. I felt like my acquired colleagues and I were brought on and that somehow we needed to be shown how to behave differently because our previous way of doing things was not valued. Our skills, abilities, contributions, and previous successes weren't always acknowledged or welcomed, and that prevented us from feeling like we were a part of the new company's community. It's one thing to take one for the team, but it has to be coupled with the extension of a sincere and gracious welcome by leadership to become part of a new community of employees.

Values, combined with that welcome and acknowledgement, help build the layer of community. When employees feel they are a part of a community, they experience a sense of belonging. The feeling of belonging to something new will help employees engage in the necessary work of integration more quickly because they will feel that they have a reason for being a part of the new company. This will help them quickly engage in the necessary work of integration and, in the longer term, they will see the opportunity to become valued members of the team.

Belonging

The third layer of the dessert is belonging. The hands and minds of employees will be productive faster when their hearts are connected to the new company. This layer of your culture dessert is the most delicious to your preferred guests. The feeling of belonging is something we all seek as human beings. When we feel like we belong in our workplace, we are far more likely to have a sense of satisfaction in our work and to want to give discretionary or additional effort to accomplish our goals.

As a business owner or executive, wouldn't you want your employees to give their best efforts as soon as possible? Wouldn't you want to them to have the feeling of being a part of building a successful organization? Over the years, I have become a big fan of NFL football. When I think about the success of my favourite NFL football team, the San Francisco 49ers, I am reminded that they too had a strategy/theme that brought them five Super Bowl championships in 13 years during the 1980s and 1990s. Their owner during those successful years was Eddie DeBartolo, Jr. DeBartolo and his family were successful business owners and ventured into owning sports franchises in the late 1970s. DeBartolo took a losing football team and helped create one of football's greatest championship dynasties. His strategy was to treat his players and staff like family by doing everything first class. He provided them with state-of-the-art training facilities and premium-quality food, travel, and accommodations. He did this because he wanted them to *feel* like they were family. The players and coaches, in turn, believed they were family, and wanted to do their best to achieve their goal— winning championships as a family. One player described this environment as having *"a fraternal sense of commitment to the organization"* (Barlow & Cossrow, 2011). DeBartolo's transformation equation for the 49ers was very simple. First class + family = success and five Super Bowl championships. Your invitation, the welcome to the new company, and how you set your table to prepare your employees for the work of pre-transformation will ultimately determine if you can actualize the goal of transformation.

Create a sense of belonging within your employee base by

having them work on common and meaningful goals. Ensure your line-leaders and executive team stay connected, and ensure an ongoing focus on driving towards the new company's goals and outcomes. During the pre-transformation phase, your employees will need to see clear ways of how they can belong to the new company. They will look for ways they can commit to the new company. Focusing them on the work and staying connected by showing care and concern will impact their sense of belonging. Belonging is the pivotal middle layer of your dessert and the one they will crave the most. Make sure you have thought through some of the ways you and the executive team can create a sense of belonging in your employee base. Those ways should be practical, so that your executive team and line-leaders can stay connected with employees and build commitment and belonging.

Opportunity

The fourth layer of this dessert is opportunity. When you invite people to come to your home for a dinner party, they will come with expectations that it will be good. There is a level of anticipation and excitement about the evening ahead. Guests will always talk with each other after a grand dinner party. The impression made by your invitation, table setting, and the courses you serve will leave a lasting imprint on them. They will talk about it amongst themselves and others. They will tell others whether or not it was good and whether they want to do it again. What is the purpose or outcome of going through the process of planning and implementing these steps?

The outcome is about seizing and creating opportunity. The opportunity to transform can be elusive but it is obtainable if values, community, and belonging are established first. When employees know why they have been brought together, have a clear plan on what needs to be accomplished, and have the tools to do so, they tend more often than not to create successful outcomes for their organizations. The opportunity layer is twofold. It speaks to the fundamental purpose of your merger or acquisition—seizing the business opportunity ahead. Improving your business results and creating sustainability and growth are key outcomes for any merger or acquisition. It also represents the opportunities for your employees to further their own careers using their existing and newly found skills, talents, and abilities to move the company forward.

I have had the good fortune of working in an environment where I felt equipped and able, and wanted to do great work. The feeling of contributing to the success of your company is very satisfying. It's even more satisfying if you believe in the company's values and see them at play in your workplace and you feel that you belong to a community of workers who are willing to put in their best efforts to grow the company and themselves.

Growth

Growth is the final layer of this incredible culture dessert. It holds the proverbial icing on the cake and is the ultimate outcome business owners and executives seek. A merged or acquired organization has truly transformed when it can clearly point to economic growth that is achievable, sustainable, and has a highly engaged workforce. True transformation is a simple equation. Clear, common goals and shared outcomes + accountability + heart = transformation. As your business begins to transform, the opportunities for growth will emerge.

How and when you seize those opportunities will depend on the soundness of the corporate strategy, how nimble and change-ready the business is, and of course, the will of the marketplace. Creating the opportunity for employees to grow personally and professionally is a positive choice business owners and executives can make. A merger or acquisition provides ample opportunity for growth! Encourage them to share their ideas on how the company can grow in sustainable ways. Help your employees grow their careers by engaging them in the future and in the transformation of the company.

Transformation

So how does this grand dinner party end? Whether you are organizing a grand dinner party or a complex merger or acquisition, some fundamental activities are the same. Both need to have a plan, both require being purposeful in how you will execute the plan, and in both cases, there is real value in creating a sense of belonging with your employees or dinner party guests. Culture, like dessert, should serve as a pleasing and ongoing memory or representation of a great experience. Your guests and the organization should be transformed by experiencing it. If it is delicious and satisfying, it caps off a fabulous evening and your guests will want to experience it over and over again!

Don't get left behind in old ways of thinking about mergers or acquisitions. No longer are they business transactions where employees and key stakeholders are an afterthought. Start planning for transformation success early during the transaction phase. Plan your party wisely so you can achieve the transformation you seek. Ensure your new company is off to a great start by engaging a Transformation Consultant today!

Your grand dinner party and guests await!

"Look at the deal holistically and consider the impacts of culture. Know the rules of the game."

– Donna Garbutt, CEO, Maxxam Analytics

Key Insights

- Culture is powerful and it resonates with employees for a long time.

- Plan for the new culture you want employees to experience at the *beginning* of any merger or acquisition transaction.

- Inspire and engage your employees. Embed the values and aspirations of the merger and acquisition you are planning. Create a dessert that they will want to enjoy over and over again.

ACKNOWLEDGEMENTS

To My Dinner Party Guests,

I extend a sincere thank-you to the business executives I interviewed. Thank you for sharing your merger and acquisition experiences and knowledge. Your insights were invaluable and provided me with a variety of perspectives on the employee experience in mergers and acquisitions, and helped validate many of the recommendations within this book.

Donna Garbutt, Chief Executive Officer, Maxxam Analytics

As Chief Executive Officer, Donna is responsible for overall leadership of Maxxam across Canada, with a strong emphasis on growing the business in line with Bureau Veritas' 2020 Strategic Plan. She brings over 25 years' experience in the oil and gas industry and a proven track record for delivering excellence in business development, key account management, strategic marketing and operations management to her role.

Donna's career has included a wide range of positions, covering many geographic markets. In most recent years, she held senior and executive management positions at Schlumberger, the world's largest oilfield services company, including President of Schlumberger Canada.

Donna currently serves as a member of the Government of Canada's Science, Technology and Innovation Council (STIC).

Margot M. Micallef, Q.C., President, Oliver Capital Partners

Margot M. Micallef, Q.C. is the President of Oliver Capital Partners, a company she founded in 2003 to invest in private companies looking for expansion capital or an outright sale. Since its inception Oliver Capital Partners has directly and indirectly invested in a number of diverse businesses including: broadcasting, publishing, food manufacturing and real estate and manages or has managed the franchise development rights for a number of well-known quick service restaurant brands including Domino's Pizza, Subway and Taco del Mar. Under Margot's leadership Oliver has returned an ROI of up to 400% to its investors.

Margot has also served as an Adjunct Professor in governance and ethics for the MBA Program at the University of Alberta and is on the Faculty of the Directors College, a joint venture between McMaster University and the Conference Board of Canada.

Perry Schuldhaus, President, Enbridge Income Fund Holdings Inc. (ENF)

Perry Schuldhaus is the President of ENF, he is responsible for overseeing and managing all aspects of the Fund's business. He has previously held the positions of Vice President, Upstream Business Development & Acquisitions, Vice President, Business Development and Director, Market Development & Acquisitions. All of these prior positions were with Enbridge Pipelines Inc., a wholly owned subsidary of Enbridge Income Partners LP. Mr. Schuldhaus holds a Bachelor's Degree in Engineering from the University of Alberta and has completed the comprehensive Finance for Senior Executives program at the Harvard Business School. In September 2015, he was invested as an Honorary Colonel in the Royal Canadian Air Force.

Heather Eddy, M.Sc., CHRP, Senior Human Resources Professional

Heather Eddy is a human resources executive with over 25 years of comprehensive experience in human resources. She has a proven track record in partnering with senior executives in the oil and gas industry to deliver value to the business. Currently she is the President of a consulting firm providing a variety of services to executives in a number of industries. Prior to this, she held senior management positions leading global human resource organizations in the oil and gas industry. She successfully co-led the change management, organizational design and selection for the Petro-Canada/Suncor merger, the largest merger in Canadian energy history, and led all of the human resources aspects of Suncor's divestiture of its natural gas assets. Over the years, Heather has been actively involved in a significant number of mergers, acquisitions, and divestitures in Canada and internationally.

My experience of the merger between Petro-Canada and Suncor ignited a passion in me that had always been there but hadn't yet met with the impetus to spark it. That passion is the desire to transform leaders, employees, and the ways in which they work together. The power of employee engagement is real and the potential to transform employees and the companies they work for is the reason I started writing this book. The personal transformation I experienced over the last four years researching and developing this book would not have been possible without the time, guidance, patience, and inspiration of many people.

To Dawn Zentner, Mark Sonnier, Jan McMillan, Vincent Micallef, Gordon Kozak and Jason Burroughs, thank you for your candor and for sharing your own experiences with mergers and acquisitions.

A special thanks to Heather Eddy for your continued support and letting me share my thoughts and hear yours over many lunches, coffees, and libations! I appreciate your perspective and wisdom.

Many thanks to my executive coach Jan Eden for your tireless support, guidance, and hard work. You encouraged me to take a leap and write this book and helped navigate me through the process. It has been quite a journey! To my layout designer, Heather Morin, thanks for your commitment to this project. George Sellas, my illustrator, you are amazing. Thanks for making my ideas come to life in pictures. Taija Morgan, thank you so much for your recommendations and editing. I am grateful for your input. I would also like to thank Carol Crenna for your initial advice and input as it helped me crystalize the focus for the book.

To my parents: you set my very first dinner table, and showed me that through hard work and dedication, you can achieve anything. A special thanks to my mom, Pat, for her ongoing counsel and advice. Thank you to the rest of my family for cheerleading me through this process and keeping me on track. Your "how's the book coming" questions helped me stay focused and push forward.

To Adrian Bohach, thank you for your unwavering support and feedback as I worked through the many stages and concepts in the book to completion. My life is richer because you are in it.

Finally, to those who read this book, I thank you. I hope that the ideas you find within these pages inspire and encourage you to employ a mindset of invitation, and consider how you can transform your business by engaging your employees.

BIBLIOGRAPHY

Barfoot, A. (2011). *Enterprise Innovation Institute Annual Report 2011*. Georgia Tech Enterprise Innovation Center.

Barlow & Cossrow (2011). *"A Football Life" Eddie DeBartolo, Jr.* Original air date: October 24, 2012, Season 2: Episode 7.

Beiker, M., Bogardus, A. & Oldham, T. (2001). *Why Mergers Fail*. The McKinsey Quarterly, 2001:4, pp. 6-9.

Blanke, G. (2004). *Between the Trapezes, Flying into a New Life with the Greatest of Ease*. Rodale Books.

Brew, A. (2014). *Why Corporate Mergers of Equals Almost Never Work*. Forbes – Leadership Forum, June 5, 2014. http://www.forbes.com/sites/forbesleadershipforum/2014/06/05/why-corporate-mergers-of-equals-almost-never-work/#63967226400a

BusinessDictionary (2016). *Discretionary Effort*. BusinessDictionary.com, Copyright 2016 WebFinance, accessed May 10, 2016 at: http://www.businessdictionary.com/definition/discretionary-effort.html

Carroll, L. (1865). *Alice's Adventures in Wonderland*. Macmillan Publishing, United Kingdom.

Cartwright, S. (2015). *Why Mergers Fail and How to Prevent it*. QFinance, Jan 14, 2015. http://www.financepractitioner.com/mergers-and-acquisitions-best-practice/why-mergers-fail-and-how-to-prevent-it?page=1

CBC News (2009). *Suncor, Petro-Canada Announce Merger.*

CBC News, Business, March 23 2009. http://www.cbc.ca/news/ business/suncor-petro-canada-announce-merger-1.805258

Deloitte (2015). *Post-merger integration, when perfection is the enemy of good.* White Paper, Deloitte.

Derain, D. (2007). *91% of Company Mergers Fail to Deliver.* Korn Ferry Hay Group, March 26, 2007, London: UK. http:// www.haygroup.com/ro/press/details.aspx?id=10207

Kotter, J. (1996). *Kotter's 8-Step Process for Leading Change.* Kotter International. http://www.kotterinternational.com/ the-8-step-process-for-leading-change/?gclid=CjwKEAjwjca5 BRCAyaPGi6_h8m8SJADryPLhXu27L0DyxjT91WnKlsJh1_ Y3uD0k2V-pQ3c-1xQSzxoCaHrw_wcB

Lewin, K. (1947). *Lewin's Change Management Model.* NHS North West Leadership Academy.

Petro-Canada (2008). *Strength to Deliver.* Petro-Canada Annual Report. http://www.suncor.com/investor-centre/financial-reports/archived-annual-reports

Schuler, R. & Jackson, S. (2001). *HR Issues and Activities in Mergers and Acquisitions.* European Management Journal, 19:3, pp. 239-253.

Schumpter (2014). *Love on the Rocks – The Romance of a Merger of Equals Rarely Lasts.* The Economist, May 17, 2014. http:// www.economist.com/news/business/21602221-romance-merger-equals-rarely-lasts-long-love-rocks

Sher, R. (2012). *Why Half of All M&A Deals Fail and What You Can Do About It.* Forbes – Leadership Forum, March 19 2012. http:// www.forbes.com/sites/forbesleadershipforum/2012/03/19/ why-half-of-all-ma-deals-fail-and-what-you-can-do-about-it/#33e1a61b20ae

Suncor (2008). *Message to Shareholders.* Suncor Annual Report. http://www.suncor.com/investor-centre/financial-reports/ archived-annual-reports

Tait, C. (2009). *Suncor, Petrocan Need Each Other's Assets.* Financial Post, Personal Finance, May 29, 2009. http://www. financialpost.com/personal-finance/story.html?id=1644095

The Globe and Mail (2008). *Suncor defends oil sands as prices sag.* The Globe and Mail, Report on Business, October 30, 2008. http://www.theglobeandmail.com/report-on-business/suncor-defends-oil-sands-as-prices-sag/article17973748/

Torys LLP (2015). *Key Legal Considerations for Mergers and Acquisitions in Canada.* M&A Top Trends 2016. http://www. torys.com/insights/publications/2015/12/ma-top-trends-2016

Waterman, R. & Peters, T. (1980). *McKinsey 7S Framework.* The McKinsey Quarterly. http://www.mckinsey.com/business-functions/strategy-and-corporate-finance/our-insights/ enduring-ideas-the-7-s-framework

Willis, A. (2009). *Teachers nearly quadruples Petrocan stake.* Globe and Mail, February 6, 2009

ABOUT THE AUTHOR

Pauline Greenidge is a corporate and employee transformation consultant and author. As the author of *A Grand Dinner Party – Setting the Table for Mergers and Acquisitions,* she shares her unique insight, wisdom and experience as an employee during the largest energy merger in Canadian history on how to better engage and retain employees from transaction to transformation during a merger or acquisition.

Pauline is recognized for her keen ability in leading business owners and executives in seeing the value of incorporating a corporate and employee transformation plan right at the onset of any merger or acquisition transaction. The transformation plan helps businesses achieve strategic outcomes through identifying and improving employee alignment, collaboration, and engagement.

Pauline holds a Certified Human Resources Professional designation from the Canadian Council of Human Resources Associations, in addition to a Bachelor of Arts degree. In addition, her professional experience includes working in some of Canada's largest organizations, including Coca-Cola and KPMG Consulting.

For over 15 years, she has developed strong partnerships with business leaders and employees in a variety of industries. She demonstrates solid business acumen and an exceptional ability to provide responsive HR tools and solutions for her clients that specialize in employee relations, engagement, learning, development and leadership coaching.

To contact Pauline to learn more about her corporate and employee transformation products and services and how to hire her for speaking engagements, please visit her website at www.paulinegreenidge.com

Made in the USA
San Bernardino, CA
10 February 2017